STORY

FOR
LEADERS

STORY

FOR
LEADERS

First published in the United Kingdom in 2016 by
London Business Forum
38 Bartholomew Close
London
EC1A 7HP
www.londonbusinessforum.com

Cover design by Guy J Sanders
Typeset in the UK by PJ Crittenden

Produced for London Business Forum by Essential Works
www.essentialworks.co.uk

ISBN Hardback: 978-0993501104
ISBN Paperback: 978-0993501111

For my father

Bernard Pearl

1930–2015

Scientist, Dentist, Barrister, Artist,
Lover of Life and Learning.

Now that was a story.

CONTENTS

PROLOGUE

We all know how a book on story has to start. So let's begin...

Once upon a time there was a leader. Just the one. And he – for leaders were almost always men in those days – sat behind a large desk in a large office at the top of a large building. Leading meant mostly giving orders to underlings. And counting the money. And playing golf.

These were good times. Especially for the leader. And even the people under the leader were relatively content. Life was fairly ordered. They knew pretty much what was expected of them. And that their jobs would be much the same at the end of their working life as they had been at the start.

Then things got complicated.

There was a war, for a start. Then another one. While men were away fighting, women took up the slack back home. Leading was no longer a male preserve. Soon women found their way into boardrooms. And men started to moisturise.

Also, the world started speeding up. There had been an industrial revolution. And now a post-industrial one. Soon nothing was standing still. Job roles appeared and disappeared overnight. Money and markets became equally volatile. National boundaries meant less and less as the globe became, well, more global. No individual leader could hope to keep up with it all. Leading was something groups of people had to do together. Which meant collaboration. Which isn't easy.

Leading became harder. But even more necessary. An increasingly complex world left a growing number of people looking for direction and – well – meaning.

Leaders tried telling people what to do. But this didn't work anywhere near as well as it had in the past. Firstly, because the leaders themselves couldn't be clear exactly what needed to be done. And also people didn't want to be ordered around. They wanted to be engaged.

Leaders tried convincing people to follow them using the magic of facts and figures. It all became quite scientific – with graphs and pie charts. This worked for a while. It was reassuring for people to think of their leaders as experts. Until they discovered that expertise only gets you so far when the world is changing exponentially.

So leaders started talking about vision. Every leader had one. And usually they lasted about three years.

Before the leader was booted out to be replaced by a new one.

There was more and more talk about leadership. And more and more haziness about what it actually meant.

Things were looking dark.

About this time, deep in the North – of London – a young man stumbles into the field of business. He – actually I – was somewhat surprised to be there, having spent most of my previous years in the arts. Opera, theatre, music, TV, film. I thought I was destined for a career on the opera stage or the TV screen, when one day – out of the blue – the phone rang.

It was the leader of one of the world's most successful companies – can't say who – wondering if I could help them bring the creativity and connectivity of the performance world into how they thought, solved problems, came up with ideas, made relationships and did business.

Could I? I had no clue. Did I let on? Absolutely not.

'Of course', I said. And they believed me.

So I packed my belongings into a small knapsack, said farewell to the fantastic world of my youth, and headed to what they called The Real World – the land of business.

And a surprising land it was.

I was surprised by the number of companies who didn't seem to actually produce anything. By the strange jargon managers used, instead of saying what they meant. By the hours people spent in meetings not actually meeting each other. By the way people were expected to work ever longer and harder, not smarter or better.

But the biggest surprise of all was to discover how much of the so called 'real world' was actually made-up. And how few people seemed to realise this. Particularly how few leaders.

Leaders mostly thought of stories as decoration – something to jazz up a speech. They didn't realise that they were living in a world that is mostly fiction. Legal fiction, maybe. But still fiction. And in a world of fiction, the wise leader should be an expert in story.

So I started working with leaders all over the world and at all levels of business. And twenty years later I thought I'd jot down some of what I'd learned and think all leaders need to know about story.

You are holding those notes in your hand today.

What happens next?

First, take a read.

Then how the story turns out depends on you.

David
London 2015

Story for Leaders

INTRODUCTION

This book is based on the work I have been doing in businesses for the last couple of decades. And in the arts for a couple of decades before that. Hey, I started young!

It was a pleasure to write. And I hope it's a pleasure to read.

You can digest it front to back, but if you're a skimmer – and I confess I am – you'll find it easy to dip in and out.

Storytelling is a hot topic at the moment. But *telling* is only one component. Which is why the first chapter looks at the ancient roots of story and why it has been key to our evolution. I know you're probably keen to get into the practical stuff, but hang in there, this is well worth knowing.

Then we take a look at how stories work in the world – and particularly the workplace; it's crucial to understand this if you're planning to use story as a leader.

If you're on the hunt for Tips and To Dos you'll enjoy chapters 3–5 which go through how you structure story, what to put in it and finally how to do some engaging storytelling. We could end there. And if you are simply looking for a way to add oomph to your presentations and have more personal impact, you might. But the next two chapters are really the heart of the book where I encourage you to think about story not only as a way to describe the past, but as a means of shaping the future. In chapter 6 we'll meet the folk who have Future Hacked us. And in chapter 7 I'll give you a process for authoring your own future story. All good things have to come to an end, which is what we'll take a look at in chapter 8.

I know you're normally not supposed to write in books, but here it is positively encouraged. There are practices throughout and space for you to get scribbling.

Oh, and when I say leader, by the way, I don't mean someone that's extraordinary, up there on a pedestal with a big flag and curved sword. I am talking about everyday leadership. If you're the kind of person who wants to get something done and works with other people to do it, if you have a team or community that looks to you for direction or guidance, if you're trying to change the status quo or make the world a better place even in a tiny way – you're the kind of leader I mean.

Leadership is more important than ever. Leaders can help give meaning to what is happening. And that's what I think story really is – meaning making.

I am delighted if your storytelling improves as a result of this book. And even happier if your leadership does too.

THE STORY OF STORY

 Stories are essentially human. The unique ability of Homo sapiens to imagine what isn't – to create fiction – is key to our evolution. Most of us are unconsciously telling stories (including to ourselves) most of the time. Most of them are unhelpful. A leader who understands this is at a huge advantage.

Chapter 1

THE STORY OF STORY

Most of what you're thinking about the world right now didn't happen, isn't happening and won't happen.

I know. Annoying. But there it is.

If you take a peek at the conscious activity inside your head right now, you'll find a bubbling soup of thoughts about past, present and future. Thoughts. Not reality.

Our memories of the *past* are highly selective and skewed by our personal interpretations. If you doubt this, just ask an average family to discuss a recent domestic disagreement and try to agree even vaguely on who said what.

What we think about the *present* – and most of us don't spend much time actually being truly present – is highly subjective. Right now, my description of the present is that I am the creative, talented, and, yes handsome author, writing a (soon to be bestselling) book in a café. The experience of the two ladies at the adjacent table is that there is a middle-aged, arty man in cycle gear annoyingly humming to himself as he taps on his laptop, probably Facebooking when he should be out looking for a proper job! Who is right? I wouldn't like to say for sure.

And what we think about the *future*? Well that's anything from conjecture to outright fantasy. My own repertoire of future imagining lurches from horror movie to romantic comedy to dystopian sci-fi to mythical epic – like a toddler who has hold of the remote and is crazily surfing through Netflix.

Bottom line, our head is full of fiction. We're living in what Plato called the Cave. We think we are perceiving what's real when in fact we are stuck in the dark, blinkered by our limited human perceptions, while true reality happens outside, in the sunlight. What looks real, solid, truthful to us is merely a shadow cast on the wall.

It's unsettling… but cheer up.

Without this ability to fill our heads with fiction, you and I wouldn't be here at all. We certainly wouldn't be having this conversation. If we had survived on Earth at all, we'd probably be languishing at the bottom of the food chain, taking orders from the Woolly Mammoth.

A key to our (hi)story

The unique ability of Homo sapiens to imagine what isn't – to create an imagined reality – is key to our evolution. More than the opposable thumb. More even than the ability to communicate in language.

Most creatures – and our ancient ancestors were no different – spend their lives in an eternal present dealing with *what is*.

I am hot? I pant.

I am hungry? I eat.

There's nothing to eat? I hunt.

Or steal your food.

I don't imagine creatures we shared the world with 100,000 years ago smarting because they were not loved enough, gossiping about the relationships in the pack, or putting money into pensions for their retirement. They dealt with what was happening. They woke, they ate, they mated and they went to sleep. (OK, there are female readers out there who think I have just described the average 21st century man, but let's move on).

This stimulus/response served our co-inhabitants of Earth well. But it had its limits, particularly in terms of scale. A small pack of animals can operate around see it-do it, but if you want to organise on a larger scale, enrol thousands, sway millions, align a species, you need something more.

You need to be able to imagine what you cannot taste, touch or feel, right here, right now. You have to be able to picture what's beyond your immediate environment, the land over the horizon, beyond the rainbow, over the sea. Then you can create unseen gods to explain away worrying phenomena like lightning and drought, sunrise and sunset, birth and death. And you can start to weave myths which create a shared sense of who we are, where we came from and where we are going.

With stories, you can march a nation to war against enemies we've never met, migrate to lands that no one has seen, found future cities from tiny settlements, build temples dedicated to the glory of deities in the sky whose existence can never be definitely proven.

And once you have done this – harnessed our story making quirk of the human mind to make the unreal seem real – you have access to a power that's unimaginably more potent than that of the most belligerent mammoth or sabre-toothed tiger.

Yuval Harari talks about this fictive quirk of Homo sapiens – our Cognitive Revolution as he calls it – being the key factor that enabled us to take pole position in Earth's ecosystem, subjugating not only all other animal competitors, but at least five other species of human as well (*Neanderthal, Denisovan, Erectus, Soloensis* and the wonderfully named, one metre tall *Homo floresiensis*).[1]

---

[1] In his splendidly entertaining book *Sapiens* – if you haven't read it, it's worth a look.

We may have called ourselves, with characteristic lack of modesty, *Homo sapiens* (Wise Man) but given our supremacy was based on our ability to fib, *Homo fabulans* (Storytelling Man) may have been more accurate. Or just *Homo mendax*, the Liar!

Lies that bind

As Harari puts it: 'the real difference between us and chimpanzees is the mythical glue that binds together large numbers of individuals, families and groups. This glue has made us the masters of creation.'

That shared narrative glue is key to how we formed cultures from shared mythologies. Fiction is also – sparing the feelings of the devout literalists amongst us – at the root of religion. Religious stories are a wonderful way to imagine away the troubling and unexplainable and so bind large numbers of disparate people into much more controllable aggregates. If in doubt, remember the word religion derives from the Latin *religare* meaning *to bind*.[2]

Shared stories create bonds across generations, across territories, across languages and continents. They are also key to our personal identities. We are our stories. Our names reflect this, whether it's a family name that suggests an ancestral occupation (Teller, Miller, Thatcher), or a patronymic (Ivanovich – son of John in

---

[2] I wonder if the binding quality is why they sometimes call stories *yarns*…

Russia or Jónsson in Iceland), a matronymic (in the Philippines you'd take your mother's first name as your middle name), a feudal appellation (…of Gaunt, …the bearded, …of the House of Tudor) or a colourful, nature inspired description such as Native Americans might use (like the Sitting Bull, Red Cloud, Crazy Horse or, a personal favourite of mine, the Crow name *Arapoosh* which translates as *stomach ache*). Your name is – more accurately – the name you were given. Given to you by a previous generation with a specific thought, reason, hope or prayer in mind. Each of our names – or nicknames – is something we have acquired. They give a clue to the lineage of which we are part, the narrative that we are living.

If you had a diary when you were a teenager you may remember how recording your day-to-day story helped form your sense of self. Physical diaries have largely been replaced today by the global obsession with Facebook. I thought it was interesting when in 2011 Facebook added a Timeline to the users profile – a program which selects posts from previous years and plays it back to you as a narrative sequence, as though to remind users they are living out a story. As Mark Zuckerberg himself points out: 'Users are keeping up with their friends and family, but they're also building an image and identity for themselves, which in a sense is their brand.' It's 21st century technology. But an ancient human need.

Businesses do the same. Click the 'who we are' button

on a corporate website and you'll get a narrative, the story of who we've been, how we got here and, sometimes, where we are going next.

Stories enable us to imagine what is not. And to imagine ourselves as we are not. As Laurens van der Post put it, so poetically:

It's the not-yet in the now, the taste of the fruit that does not-yet exist, hanging the blossom on the bough.[3]

OK, so fiction making may be the evolutionary reason we are here, but what does this have to do with today? How does this anthropological insight help us now? What links our hairy storytelling ancestors to us sophisticated 21st century types? Fiction making was clearly important to cavemen, terrified the sun would never rise in the morning, but in the intervening centuries, surely reality has got more solid and predictable?

Er, no. If anything, what's real has never been more up for grabs. And this is rather unsettling to the organisations I work with and those that lead them.

I personally discovered the wobbliness of reality long before I started work. The hard way.

I was nine, walking my seven-year-old brother to school. I think of it as the day Reality Got Run Over.

---

[3] In *Venture to the Interior.*

Physically it was my brother (now a happy and successful lawyer) who got hit by the car. But in my mind, when I look back on it now, it was 'reality' that was scooped onto the bonnet of the unlicensed, stolen car and scrunched into the parked van.

The accident came out of a clear blue sky. A moment before Jonathan and I were counting pavement cracks. The next it was broken glass and blue flashing lights.

Several painful operations later, Jon was up and about, impressing friends with his waist to toe plaster cast and some truly dramatic head scars. But my sense of reality never really recovered. Certainty about the future remained lying at the road side. Not that this was bad news. In a way, this horrible low point (we'll talk more about these later) taught me something invaluable...

Reality isn't as real as they say it is. It can be turned on its head in a squeal of brakes. And somewhere in my head a small voice asked the question: 'If such bad things can happen unexpectedly, can't extraordinarily beautiful ones happen without warning too?' I become less trustful of the reality experts. *It's real? Says who?* My sense of the predictable took a real blow to the head. 'Never mind what everyone says will happen in the future – what do I want to make happen?'

That experience has shaped my life in very helpful ways. I wish it hadn't happened – but as it did – I am really grateful for it. It was only when I sat down to write this book that I really appreciated the unbroken line that connects that glass-strewn London side street to the work I do now, helping businesses and those that lead them shape reality through the stories they tell – and live.

The power of story goes far beyond entertaining each other round a campfire. It is how we create the world. And while it may be troubling for some people to realise how much of our lives are pure make-believe, for you, as a leader, it's gold dust.

How so?

Because story gives you a key to performance

A lot of leaders I meet complain their teams lack energy. If you are one, ask yourself: 'How meaningful is the work I am asking people to do?' Meaningless work is very hard to get excited about. And yet it needs to be done. It's tempting to start thinking about incentives or threats. But the minute you remember that all meaning is constructed, you have another way in. Create a worthwhile story and even menial tasks become meaningful. Your job is not to trick people into doing meaningless work – but to make work meaningful. Less directive, more narrative. If you have director in your job description, then direct – like a film director would.

Because story keeps you sharp

A leader who thinks about the stories they are *telling* will be more aware of the stories being told to *them*.

Stories, remember, are brilliant ways of putting us to sleep. Ask any parent of a restless toddler. Right now, in your organisation, people are telling you stories designed to make you close your eyes and slumber. Stories about why things are impossible, why deadlines are unattainable, about why you should accept less than the best. Some of the most incisive leaders I know cut straight through these blocking facts. They know it's just blocking fiction.

Because story makes it easier to change things

The leaders I work with are all, in their way, trying to influence change: culture, attitude, performance, results, mindset. In one way or another, their job is to upset the status quo. The trouble is the status quo often bites back, putting all sorts of obstacles in the way. *It can't be done! We tried before and failed! There isn't the money/time/resources. It'll never work!* And these can look very compelling. But a leader who views this as a giant game of 'Let's Pretend' isn't going to be so easily stumped; that leader won't let facts get in the way of the reality they want to create. Facts are just fictions that have been around long enough to seem real.

Al Gore knows a lot about how people will try to block facts they don't like with ones they do. He's a leader who hasn't let the so called 'factual' evidence of the climate change deniers stand in the way of the opinion-shaping environmental story he intends to tell:

When you have the facts on your side, use the facts. When you have the law on your side, use the law. When you have neither – holler!

It's the same when someone brandishes figures to try and stymie a committed leader. 'All figures are either looked up or made up', a senior business leader once confided to me. 'And those that are looked up – are made up.'

And when blocked by the hackneyed *'there's not enough money'*, leaders usually find it. They know that budgeting is largely a fictional process, the financial power at your disposal is more to do with the confidence you create than the hard cash you hold.

And while a lot of us are put off by tackling 'the system' – the most skilled leaders I have seen in action act as though the system was created once and therefore can be recreated. For them, an organisation isn't a structure in the mechanical sense. It's an agreement – a shared fiction. Organisations look far more solid to those that work in them than they do to those who made them up in the first place. Ask a founder. They remember when the global corporation of today was just an idea round a kitchen table or a prototype in a garage.

I always used to enjoy seeing Michael Dell in action. He seemed, well, more relaxed than the people around him. I can't help feeling it had something to do with the fact that Dell, the global computing corporation of today, started on a hunch as a venture in his college dorm room.

Anyone arguing for the solidity of the modern organisation just needs to see how frequently and with what ease they are reorganised. When another restructure is announced – and it can be several times a year these days – no-one sets to with power tools to physically re-engineer anything. Premises don't need to be bought or sold. Hoardings are not necessarily reworded or repainted. Change can be effected at the stroke of a CEO's pen because there is nothing physical *to* change. Titles on business cards may be reworded but roles often stay pretty similar.[4] Restructuring happens in our minds. Because that's where businesses – even very big businesses – actually exist.

By the way, those massive corporations that have colonised the globe and seem so real, actually *are* fictions. Legal fictions.

The story is this. Once upon a time, the law said if you were unhappy with a product or service you could sue a person. But only a person. That was fine when all you had was wheelwrights and blacksmiths. If the wheel fell off your oxcart, or your horse threw that new shoe, you'd have a legitimate claim against the artisan who did the work. Then along came the Industrial Revolution. Things got noisier, busier and a lot more complex. Suddenly large groups of people were setting up companies. But you

---

[4] Of course people often lose their jobs. So I wouldn't argue restructuring doesn't have real consequences. Just that the structure being reformed is essentially a mental concept that exists as long as we all agree it does.

couldn't sue a company, remember, only a person. What to do? Somewhere a nifty lawyer squared the circle and argued a group of people could 'incorporate' – that is, become a single body. These huge new corporations, so called, were now effectively a *person*. I am not making this up. The lawyers did. And the far-fetched legal fiction of 'corporate personhood' remains one of the dominant underpinnings in the business reality of today.

Because story helps leading be less arduous

Think of all the time you spend convincing people you are right. And all the energy that goes into justifying what you've done. It's like trying to shift a heavy weight up a hill. When you approach life – especially working life – as though it's made up, you can stop battling your people's reality. You recognise it for what it is, a story. And concentrate on creating a more helpful story. This mindset is a lot less debilitating than the 'I am right you are wrong' approach. My friend the über consultant Michael Breen once saw me struggling with a concept of his that I found hard to believe: 'Don't waste time figuring out whether this is true or not' he chuckled, 'treat everything I say as fiction. And just ask yourself if it's a useful fiction or not'.

It's downright freeing. Try it.

Because story gives you a helpful 'heads up'

When you see life as a story, and that includes history, you'll have a better idea of what's coming. The future isn't impenetrable when you see that all stories have the same elements. In different orders perhaps, and with different nuance and emphasis, but predictable nonetheless. When you're watching a thriller or reading a love story, you have a pretty good idea of how it's going to turn out and at least some of what's going to happen along the way. The basic geometry of story has been hardwired into us. And it's the same with the stories we are living. When you start looking at a project more as a narrative arc and less like an arrow-straight plan, you'll have a much better idea of what lies ahead on the landscape of the future. We'll read more about signposts later in the book. Given that those elements are inevitable, you can start preparing creative responses to them well in advance.

Because life becomes more fulfilling and more fun

Too often leaders become trapped in being managers. Their lives become operational, not inspirational. And inspiration is what leaders are for. When you think of yourself as a story maker – that is, a creator of meaning – your job description changes radically.

The world is going through a meaning drought at this stage of our history. When you are thinking 'meaning' not just 'action' you're making a valuable contribution, irrespective of your job, pay grade or industry sector. Some of the most impressive leaders I've met are not at all celebrated or eminent. They don't swagger through the corridors of power or lounge on the padded leather thrones of the c-suite. They're local heroes. They are leaders in the trenches of life who think about making life more meaningful for those they lead, enriching lives through the stories they are telling – and living.

And because it's your duty

At least, I'd argue it is. As we've seen in this chapter, our stories create a context which shapes our thought and action. Humans have always been especially prone to a good story. The trouble is most of the stories are not 'good'. And that, at this period of our development, has helped bring our race into something of a pickle.

Just take a look at the stories people tell currently, about the world, about each other, about themselves. The stories of 'might is right', 'for me to win, you must lose', of 'it's impossible to solve', of 'poor little me', of 'we are owed and they are not'. Listen carefully to those centuries-old stories, the ones that every generation returns to create new enemies of neighbours. Notice the toxic fables that turn children into warriors, which distract groups, companies, populations, even the whole species, from doing what they know is right.

Right now people are spreading narratives designed to agitate, inflame or unsettle us. Just turn on the media. Others, and there are some splendid proponents in politics, religion and advertising, are cooing their soothing tales designed to get us to nod off.

This is why leadership is more important than ever.

When you see how many of our human stories are unhelpful, I'd say you have an obligation NOT to add to them.

If you think of yourself as a leader of others, then creating inspiring stories and helping realise them is a central part of your role.

It may not be in your job description but if you are working for an organisation, or leading one, you have a responsibility to manage its stories. Not only the brand story it tells about itself, but the story that shapes its character and actions.

If you have the gift of language and the privilege to use it freely, create the kind of stories you want people to tell about you after you.

Our species has a unique ability to *imagine* the world other than it is. It's time to use it to *create* a world other than it is.

FIRST, TRY THIS…

Practice #1: How did you get here?

Leaders create meaning. Not just in the epic moments, but in the everyday ones. Especially the everyday ones – because there are a lot more of them!

In other words, story making is not just a technique you need to practise for formal presentations. They are relatively straightforward. And your audience will be expecting it. What's powerful is when you spot the opportunity to enrich the meaning of what's happening at times and in ways they don't anticipate.

Here's a practice to hone your ability to do this in the most ordinary of situations.

How did you get here?

It seems such a simple question. A pleasantry. Something people ask without expecting an interesting answer.

And it's tempting to answer it in a simple, factual way. 'By cab… I walked… I took the lift from the 9th floor'.

Job done. Question answered. Move on.

But wait.

You can see it as a request for information or the opportunity for a story. They have just asked you about your *journey* to here. How you answer depends on when you consider that journey started.

Try this practice and I think you'll find 'how did you get here?' is actually a wonderful cue for a story.

How did you get here? Right here, where you are now – reading this book, wherever you are reading it.

Please answer the question in no more than 100 words starting your account three minutes ago:

_____

_____

_____

_____

_____

_____

_____

_____

_____

Then do it again, starting from your first day at school:

_____

_____

_____

_____

_____

_____

_____

_____

_____

Then again, starting a century ago (so including your ancestors):

_____

_____

_____

_____

_____

_____

_____

_____

_____

Now one final time, starting at the Big Bang:

_____

_____

_____

_____

_____

_____

_____

_____

_____

Notice how much more power there is in the present when you remember what led up to it. Notice what details you choose to include – or discard – when you have the same number of words to describe a few minutes and hundreds of thousands of years. As a storyteller, you're like a film director focusing on the details you want the audience to notice.

Clearly you may not choose to answer every day-to-day question with a story. I certainly wouldn't advise it. But do notice how even seemingly uninteresting questions are an opening for you to respond with something more enriching.

And how might you apply this directly to the business situation? Consider how often you encounter a person, or a room full of them, who want you to answer this question, or a variant of it:

- How did we get here?
- What progress has been made?
- Where did this product, company, idea come from?
- Who are you and why should I be listening to you?
- Why do you think you are right for this job?

These are all essentially invitations for you to describe the *journey to here*. You can give them the plain information. Or you can create a story. One is going to have far more impact than the other.

STORIES @ WORK

 You need to know how stories are at work in your business. Or these stories can stop your business working! It's time to meet the Three Fs; they are stories that have colonised most organisations and which the leader needs to overwrite.

Chapter 2

STORIES @ WORK

'If you're leading and no-one's following', goes the ancient Mongolian saying, 'you're just going for a walk.'

Quite. Leadership has become a buzzword. Many of us are called leaders but how many of us actually think of ourselves that way? They insert the word into our job titles – Team Leader, Business Leader, Thought Leader, Opinion Leader – but the only way to really know if it's deserved is if you're being actively followed. I say *actively* because if you are a boss, business owner, or senior executive, a certain amount of followership is a given. People will, by and large, do what they are told if their job and salary depend on it. Active following is something else, something that a lot of my clients are desperate to create.

How do you get people to follow you? Especially when times are hard, challenges are harder and changes keep coming thick and fast?

Incentives are helpful but they'll only get you so far – as anyone who has seen highly paid employees defect or underperform will tell you. Yes, it's important to keep people informed, to be transparent, to empower them and give them the tools to do their job. Integrity, authenticity, credibility are all powerful assets. But if you want to engage people, especially a lot of them, I'd suggest nothing trumps the ability to create a meaningful narrative.

The times we are living through are information rich, meaning poor. We're overwhelmed with competing messages. There's so much coming at us so fast, making sense of it all is like trying to sip from a fire hose.

We binge on data but we're still hungry for meaning. Meaning brings energy, even to mundane tasks. Like the NASA janitor, in the eternally-quoted story, who tells JFK he is putting a man on the moon.[1]

And that's why storytelling – what I call meaning-making – is such a key skill for a leader. When you change people's story of the world, you change everything.

---

[1] A personal plea here. If you are tempted to tell that story in a presentation or speech, please don't. Everyone, but everyone has heard it! Or, if you can't resist, tell them what the janitor really replied: '*What does it look like I am doing, Mr President? I am sweeping the floor. Idiot!*'

The inventor of NLP, Richard Bandler, used to tell us students: 'You can change the world or you can change how you see the world. And one is a lot easier than the other.'

Here's a beautiful example of a leader doing just that.

The Eden Project is something of a miracle. It's a jewel of biodiversity that erupts out of a once disused quarry in Bodelva, Cornwall, under futuristic biomes like giant flies eyes. It is such a good idea, so self-evidently a good thing for the county, tourism, the environment, the economy, and our national prestige that it's hard to imagine someone not seeing the potential.

But the visionary Tim Smit, whose brainchild it was, tells of the innumerable obstacles that had to be overcome to make this happen.

It was early in the project's life and the wildly ambitious concept had progressed as far as elbow grease, good will, lots of blagging and huge dollops of optimism could take it. Now Tim realised he needed a serious, multi-million pound injection of funds or the project would wither on the proverbial vine. Fortunately this coincided with the first round of funding awards by the newly created National Lottery. One-time rock musician-turned-environmental activist, Tim had never applied for funding of any kind. Undeterred, he pulled together the business plan, filled out the forms, and bought a fax machine to receive the award he was certain would arrive. How could the Lottery not see what Tim and all his supporters could, that this was an idea that absolutely deserved backing to the hilt?

On the great day, everyone crowded round the fax machine as it whirred into life to announce – tragic news. The Lottery hadn't awarded the grant. You could argue this wasn't completely unreasonable. Tim and his friends were making a multi-million pound request for a brand new project nobody had heard of. But the Lottery had a second level award, one where they withheld the money but gave encouragement and recommended a re-application.

But Eden hadn't even received a provisional yes. It was a flat no. Zip. Nada.

End of story?

Yes, at that point most of us would have given up. But Tim Smit ordered champagne! And a bath full of ice to put it in. Then he rang up everyone he knew and invited them over for a party. Press included. At the climax of the shindig he stood up to toast the Lottery for the wisdom of their choice. He never actually said they had awarded the funding to the Eden Project. He let the audience make that assumption. When the story went out nationally the Lottery were understandably surprised. But also flattered. Not only was Tim complimenting them on their vision and daring. So were countless pundits and members of the public up and down the country. They hastily reconsidered their original choice and not long afterward the Eden Project's fax machine was whirring again. This time with the money.

What I love about this anecdote is the way Tim Smit refused to accept the premise of defeat. He didn't argue with the Lottery, plead his case, seek to alter their narrative. He didn't try to rewrite their story (the Eden Project is a crackpot idea that doesn't deserve public money) he OVERwrote it with one of his own. And told it more compellingly and more publicly. It was simply a better story. And, on reflection, the Lottery funders agreed.

Why is this helpful for you as you navigate the highs and lows of your own working life? Because, like Tim Smit, you are going to encounter resistance, particularly if you ever seek to do anything bold, ambitious, counter-cultural or out of the ordinary. Yes, you will find persuasive storytelling is going to be a potent way of meeting that resistance. But there's a hidden trap. The people you are engaging will already have a story sitting in their mind, shaping their view of the world. And they generally won't want to let go of it! Along you come, with your bright, shiny new idea and fresh thinking. Your story makes perfect sense to you. To them, you are an anomaly. A foreign body. Alarm bells ring. Fences go up. Immune systems activate. Paper-knives are sharpened. The politics begin.

As a story maker at work, the leader is NOT writing on a blank sheet. Your audience is pre-loaded with their own narratives. If your version of reality is to take hold, you first have to replace theirs with something more vibrant, vital and energising.

Which is why I wanted to give you a 'heads up' about three of the most persistent macro stories of business. I have found them deeply embedded in most of the organisations I have worked with. And I won't pretend otherwise – you are going to need your authoring skills if you are going to uproot them.

The Three Fs

Every business I have ever met – every organisation and, come to that, family – has its stories. And these stories – from gossip to epic – co-exist in, what I like to think of as, a story ecosystem. A Brain Forest, if you will. It's a survival of the fittest type place. A delicate, interconnected web where some stories flourish and others struggle. As a leader this is the terrain you need to navigate. And when you have a new story to tell, it's like you are introducing a bright new life-form – a fluffy bunny of potential – into a wild that's full of predators. Hungry ones.

Have a care.

For the ecosystem of most companies has been colonised by three big stories, the Giant Redwoods of the Brain Forest so to speak, that are so well established and so strong they deprive newcomers of the light and nutrients they need to take hold.

I think of them as the Three Fs: Fear, Fantasy and Formula. Know them well. Learn to recognise them in the gossip at the watercooler, the strangely resistant attitudes of colleagues, the barbed comments at the sales meeting. If your own story is going to be successful, it must compete for light and nutrients with these alpha narratives.

Fear

There's nothing wrong with a bit of fear. It's been installed in us as a check mechanism to keep us safe, alert and alive. It's smart to be frightened of high cliffs, hissing snakes and bushfire. Let's say yes to fear when it's 'mature and fully embodied', as Zen master and inventor of the Big Mind Movement, Genpo Roshi, says. That's the kind of fear that we want. Let's fear inequality. Let's fear mediocrity. Let's fear stupidity.

Properly harnessed, fear can be very useful. And enjoyable. Scary stories aren't just an entertaining way to while away a night around the fire; they are a time-honoured means of passing on important learning. For instance, don't go into a maze to kill a monster without unwinding a ball of string so you can find your way out. Don't trust the talking snake; it is going to end badly …

But as an operating system for daily or organisational behaviour, fear-based stories are not recommended. They clog progress, rob new ideas of oxygen, keep us stuck.

You'll know fear stories are operating in the background of a company whenever you hear phrases like: *it'll never work… we tried that already… where will we get the money… ask the lawyers… there are going to be job losses… we've always done it that way…*

41

Fear-based stories keep us what I call Future Tense, jumping at shadows, convinced destruction waits round every bend. They usually start with the word '*but*'. And they all end in the promise of misery, failure, shame, loss, horror and/or death.

A client I am working with currently – one of the UK's most potent financial institutions – is under new, enlightened management. But the fear stories of the past are deep-rooted. On the surface the mood is upbeat. But lurking in the undergrowth is the old, old story: 'Mess up and you're dead.' It creates obsessive consensus, sluggish decision making and leaden bureaucracy as people – understandably – seek to survive by not failing or, more importantly, distributing blame for the inevitable failures when they come. It's a perfectly reasonable code for survival in the storyland they inhabit.

Paradoxically, though fear stories are everywhere in organisations, they are also invisible, hidden, unexpressed. That outwardly confident, often strident boss who seems scared of nothing but scares others? Her inner story is pure fear. Talking about fear – telling the scary story that's running behind your eye? Well, it's just not done. Which is a shame, because shining a light on these stories, exposing them to oxygen, is the quickest way to rob them of their toxic power.

Nelson Mandela knew this when, as soon as he took power in South Africa, he set up the Truth and

Reconciliation Commission, not to punish the guilty but to allow them publicly to share their stories of guilt without threat of reprisal. He talks specifically about the detoxifying effect of expressing these stories, when receiving the TRC report in 1998:

> *We should pay tribute to the 20,000 men and women who relived their pain and loss in order to share it with us; the hundreds who dared to open the wounds of guilt so as to exorcise it from the nation's body politic; exorcising a past which threatens to live with us like a festering sore.*

You don't have to be a Head of State to apply the principle, by the way. Boe Hartman, the Chief Information Officer at Barclaycard, told me about the day he 'outed' fear in his organisation:

> *We'd been doing OK in my part of the business but we were stuck. People weren't really performing as they could. Me included. As a way to get things moving, I thought I would do something quite shocking and that was to share my own end of year review, warts and all.*

Boe, I should explain, is something of a maverick. Born dyslexic and poor, he grew up on a horse farm in Virginia chopping his own firewood. His path to the corporate top table has been unconventional. And that's a key to his leadership style. The industry he is working in is known as 'one of the toughest on the planet' where transparency is a rarity. 'People tend to prey on weakness and typically leaders keep their vulnerability covered.'

So people weren't prepared when Boe laid out his shortcomings so publicly:

The first big meeting was in India. I took people through the detail of my performance review, really focussing on where I thought I had failed to perform. No-one had spoken to them like this before. They wanted to support me and make polite, reassuring noises but I pushed on telling them, this is a picture of someone who is not leading the way, who is failing to represent your work powerfully, who is holding the organisation back.

But why was I doing this? I didn't even know myself until I said it.

'Because I am scared.'

Everyone in the room was stunned. Me included. It was like the air had been sucked out of the room. I had never said this before, never thought it; not through the poverty or the dyslexia. But when I did, I felt my shoulders relax and gave a big sigh. I looked around and my head of HR, a hardened professional had tears in her eyes.

I feared I wasn't smart enough, that I was going to fail. I was scared of a story that's not real, that exists only in my head. But that fear was holding back the potential of the entire organisation.

This one phrase went round the organisation like wildfire. At the end of the meeting and for months after, people were thanking me for admitting my fear. It made them realise it was OK for them to be afraid too.

The effect on the business was transformative. Every single metric a business could use to assess our performance – customer impact, system stability, cost efficiency, productivity – not only went up, we blew the doors off. We did things people said you couldn't do. We set up three completely new businesses while making multi-million dollar savings. One person even tried to stop us succeeding and I told him: 'You can stop me, but there are 3,000 people behind me you cannot stop'. That's the thing about outing your own fears as a leader – it creates a community around you.

Fear stories are incredibly hardy. The fact that, by and large, what we fear is going to happen doesn't actually occur, seems to do nothing to lessen our addiction. Fear stories not only persist, they grow.

The spiral of gun ownership and gun-related crime in the US is a perfect example of this.

Until the '70s, the National Rifle Association was essentially a group of hobbyists in hunting gear who clubbed together to promote gun sports and teach Boy Scouts to put bullets in a target – not in their own feet. On 21 May 1977, in what has become known as the Cincinnati Revolt, the NRA was taken over by a group of committed right-wing conspiracists with a political scare story to tell. They were – and still are – convinced the US government will confiscate everyone's guns and then impose a state tyranny, which unarmed citizens will be powerless to resist.

What is really scary is that the USA bought it. Today, the NRA is one of the most powerful and feared lobbying groups in Washington and preventing anyone owning a deadly firearm – even those with a history of mental illness – is seen as a violation of personal freedom.

There are now more guns than ever. Spawning more gun crime.

The chief opposition to the NRA is led by an ex-member. Two parts of the NRA are scared of each other. And everyone is scared of them.

In a horrible irony, the 2012 school slaying at Sandy Hook in Newtown, Connecticut was carried out by the son of a 'prepper', one of the growing number of Americans who are so convinced a government-initiated Armageddon is around the corner they are stocking up with food, medicine and guns. Not just any guns, we're talking military grade assault weapons.

Ask them why and they'll all somewhere cite 'defending their children'. Threat to the family or tribe is one of the most primal of our fear stories. So guns bought to defend children are being used to cut them down.

These are people locked in what looks like an unbreakable cycle of fear stories. Like guard dogs snarling at their own reflection.

The fear of being shot is trumped by the fear of not being able to shoot back. This is the 'good guy with a gun to stop a bad guy with a gun' argument that NRA apologists trot out to defend their position. It's not the gun's fault, you see, but the people wielding them. Which is true, of course. Only, if the most life-threatening weapons available were, say, ping pong paddles, my hunch is less people would die.

Fear does odd things to our sense of proportionality. The US State Department's own records show that 406,496 Americans slew each other with firearms between 2001 and 2013. In that same time a total of 3,380 citizens died through acts of terrorism around the world. Yet, while the global War on Terrorism has attracted billions of dollars and full governmental support, there has been virtually no action on the suicidal and avoidable carnage on US streets. Clearly the terrorism story trumps the mortal fear narrative. I guess that's why it has 'terror' in the title!

More guns lead to more violence which leads to more guns. After senseless mass slayings like the ones at

Columbine, Sandy Hook, Charleston and most recently Umpqua Community College – NRA support typically goes UP! The arms race isn't over. It's very much alive. And it's fuelled by an upwardly spiralling scare story.

Let's leave fear on an upbeat note, though. This, from Aung San Suu Kyi, formerly prisoner of the Myanmar government and now, at the time of writing, the country's next likely leader:

> *It is not easy for a people conditioned by fear under the iron rule of the principle that might is right to free themselves from the enervating miasma of fear. Yet even under the most crushing state machinery courage rises up again and again, for fear is not the natural state of civilized man.*[2]

Fantasy

Let's move to the second of the Three F's: Fantasy.

These are the cartoon-simple fables that optimistically assume you jump from A to Z without any intervening difficulty. You just close your eyes and wish. It's all simple, straightforward. The lovers of fantasy stories clearly didn't hear the second half of Einstein's famous quote 'make everything as simple as possible – but not too simple.'

The fantasists are like the celebrity-struck teenager

---

[2] *Freedom from Fear* by Aung San Suu Kyi.

singing into their hairbrush in a bedroom, convinced that a Grammy is on the way but with no idea of the work it entails.

CEOs are prone to fantasy statements, particularly early in their tenure, when they want to paint a primary-colour picture of where they are taking the company and how amazing it's going to look when they get there.

As we'll discuss later in the book, a leader needs to harness the power of intention, using vision to shape what comes next. That's not the same as a kind of 'hey presto' conjuring, which often turns out to be an illusion.

Fantasy comes in a range of options, from benign to life-threatening.

At the soft end are essentially day dreams. And who hasn't had them? *If I ran this place I'd… When I retire I'll… One day, they're really going to appreciate me and…* You fill in the blanks.

At least once every Sunday morning as I cycle through the North London greenbelt with my cycle buddies, I am a pro racer set to win a stage of the Tour de France. It's a short lived fantasy but so real – and so enjoyable – for the few seconds it lasts before I am overtaken by a posse of leaner, meaner weekend warriors in their dayglo lycra.

More threatening, but usually harmless, are the revenge fantasies that boil up and down the corridors of the workplace. *If he does that again I'm going to… Next time she says that, I'm going to tell her to…* These fantasies are probably quite a healthy escape valve for occupational rage – and certainly less damaging than actually riveting the boss to the photocopier with the staple gun.

At the other end of the scale is the full-on delusion; the fantasy that the fantasist no longer recognises as a fantasy. I think of Jeffrey Skilling assuring investors in February 2001 that Enron was 'the Toyota of the Energy Industry… one of the good guys…' In February he accepted the role of CEO of the business that had proclaimed itself The World's Leading Company. By August he had stepped down again. By December Enron collapsed – a 100 billion dollar mirage that evaporated with huge collateral damage. Not only was Skilling, fantasist in chief, jailed, but 4,500 employees lost their jobs and (shame) their nest eggs. Investors lost 60 billion dollars. Even advisors Arthur Andersen lost their accreditation and went out of business.

Enron is a modern morality tale that has spawned several books, a Hollywood film and even a Tony award winning musical. Fantasy can be dangerous, not only for the fantasist, but for everyone around them.

Formula

And third, obstinately chuntering through the jungle with its head down, is Formula, with only one tale to tell really. The formula story says: *If I just keep on doing what I am doing, life will leave me alone.* Stick to the knitting and everything will be ok. Formula lovers believe that what worked in the past will continue to work in the future. It's the favourite tale of the Neutrals. These are the perfectly affable types in lots of companies who pay lip service to the changes you suggest and then go back to doing exactly what they have always done. Neutrality is the polite smile that says yes and the dead eyes that say no, the cheerful 'love your idea' masking the inner conviction, *you're clearly insane*.

Formula isn't the noisiest story, but in some ways it's the most insidious.

I feel I should write more about this topic but I notice my energy has plummeted. Formula will do that to you. Rob your new idea of energy. Deaden it with the slow beat of routine.

Fear, Fantasy and Formula

They're not the only stories in the forest, by any means. Other big players in Storyland are: The Fable of Paranoia (*Don't Trust Anyone*), The Tales of Self-Doubt (*I'm out of my depth but I don't want to be found out*), and Misplaced Self-Confidence (*I'm still out of my depth and still don't want to be found out*), The Ego Myth (*It's all about me, me, ME*) and its close cousin The Epic of Insatiable Ambition (*It's never, ever enough*). But in my view they are all subordinate to the Three Fs who sit at the top of the food chain.

What makes the Three Fs such formidable blockers to change is that these are stories we tell *ourselves*. They run round the inside of our head on endless loops until we believe them.

This is why I like to think of narratives as Neuratives, as patterns of neural activity that profoundly shape our thinking. OK, it's not scientifically proven that we *become* the stories we tell ourselves – not yet – but neuroscience certainly agrees on the power of stories. As my friend, the neuroplasticity expert Tara Swart (co-author of *Neuroscience for Leadership*) was telling me:

> *Across evolution our brains have been wired to tell and listen to stories. Even before language, cave people told stories in pictures of successful hunts and so on. Because they have been around so long, stories are embedded in our ancient neural architecture, specifically the limbic system, the part of our brain that's most intuitive and instinctive.*
>
> *Stories engage both our modern logical cortex, that folded area that sits over our brain and which is mostly to do with articulated speech and planning for the future. As well as engaging us emotionally and through the limbic system.*

So narratives engage more of our minds than pure facts. And the more we tell these narratives, the more real they become:

Our brain works through interconnection. The more interconnections that occur through any activity you do, the easier that pathway is to go down and to become the default pathway; i.e. your new way of being – your story.

Neuratives don't just stay inside our heads. We project them outwards and they become filters through which we experience the world. You must have had the experience where your inner story tells you that, say, someone at work doesn't like you. Our inner sense-maker ensures everything they do or say seems additional evidence of the habitual story running between our ears.

To make it even trickier, we often beam these stories out without being aware that's what we are doing. It's classic projection – or Projektion if you're a proper Freudian – where you neatly outsource something you don't like to be in your own mind and conveniently place it in someone else's.

A leader needs to be aware that people see and hear you through the filter of their inner neuratives. You may be the hero of your own story, but you may well be the nemesis in someone else's!

So, in summary, the stories we repeatedly tell ourselves become our reality. It's a chilling thought, perhaps. But it has an exciting corollary. Because our unconscious mind doesn't know the difference between reality and a deeply imagined fiction, when we start telling more compelling narratives – sorry neuratives – to ourselves, and to others, we can change the world.

And that's where we are heading next.

! THINKING BREAK...

Practice #2: Three Fs (negative neurative)

As we've seen, it's very hard to tell someone a story when they are already telling themselves one. But that's the job of leaders. To overwrite the unhelpful story that's playing behind a person's eyes with a more helpful one.

It takes practice. You have to be able to get inside their mind. To see the world through the filter of their inner narrative. The good news is you have – quite literally – a head start. Because you've told yourself fear, fantasy and formula stories all your life.

So let's begin. And in the best place you can. Your own mind.

Think of something you'd really like to do/have/achieve and haven't. Got it? Great. Let's call it The Thing. Now I want to ask you to write three short tales about The Thing. You'll need to switch on the appropriate mood (apprehension, insane optimism, dogged moderateness).

First, jot down why you should be terrified of The Thing. And how the journey towards reaching or achieving it will be fraught with difficulties. What do you risk if it all goes wrong? Would you feel like you deserve The Thing if you finally got it?

Now, tell yourself the tale of why there's no reason to worry and it's going to be absolutely simple for a super hero like you. Piece of cake. It's your destiny and you deserve it. That kind of thing…

Finally, tell yourself why doing exactly what you are doing is the perfect strategy to get The Thing. You know. Stick to the knitting and you'll get there.

Remember, the best way to engage your audience is to understand the stories they are currently telling themselves. You do know them. Because you have told yourself the very same stories.

STORY CRAFT

 You know how to construct a plan, but how is story different? And why do stories turn people on, when PowerPoints send them to sleep? A plan is the most direct route between A and B while story is the most interesting route. 'The cat sat on the mat is not a story' said John le Carré. 'The cat sat on the dog's mat is!'

Chapter 3

STORY CRAFT

Leaders often ask me to help improve their storytelling – the way they put a narrative across. I usually start with their story writing – the way they structure the narrative they want to tell.

It's very hard – if not impossible – to tell a good story that's poorly constructed.

People are surprised when Hollywood launches yet another multi-million dollar blockbuster with a stellar cast, amazing special effects, astounding locations and huge promotion budgets – and it bombs at the box office. Stars and special effects cannot compensate for a lousy script – we need a story that really engages us.

A good narrative isn't just well told, it's well designed. You'll know this if you've ever tried to retell a joke –

really a micro story – and haven't worked out which detail goes where and how it all builds to the punch line.

Here's a joke about a Jewish grandmother. You can substitute Indian, Chinese... indeed any nationality where grannies are ambitious for their grandkids. (So that'll be any nationality then.)

> *A Jewish grandmother is walking down the street with her two grandchildren. A neighbour asks who they are and she says: 'Ruben is 11, Lewis is 13. Ruben is going to be a doctor and Lewis is going to be a lawyer.'*

Hmm. Not great, I think you'll agree. The situation is clear enough. It's mildly amusing. But it's not going to have them rolling in the aisles. The problem is not in the telling but in the construction.

Try again – this time with a different flow, choice of words and rhythm:

> *A Jewish grandmother is walking down the street with her two grandchildren. When a neighbour asks her how old they are, she replies: 'The doctor is 7, the lawyer is 5.'*

Better, right? Same basic idea, just rewritten so it's more condensed, more focused, has a punch line. It has a beginning, middle and end. I bet you get a laugh.

By the way, it probably helps to lower the ages, as I did, and reverse them to put the lower age last. Comics, particularly the ones that look most spontaneous, will often slave for hours over their material, refining until it's just right. I swear I once heard two stand ups arguing about which was the funnier number, 6 or 7. (The answer, apparently, is 7.)

Here's an example where just one word can turn a successful telling into nonsense.

The philosopher Descartes walks into a bar.

The bartender says: 'Hey, René. Gonna have your usual?'

'I don't think I am', Descartes replies.

And disappears.

If the philosopher had said 'I don't think I will' or 'I don't think so' it makes nonsense of the whole tale. Because we all associate Descartes with the phrase 'I think therefore I am', only that precise verbal formula makes the story work and funny.

Clearly not all of your storytelling needs such word-by-word precision but the message here is…

Leaders write. And rewrite.

You know the Gettysburg Address? 'Fourscore and seven years ago…' Lincoln was apparently scribbling amendments with a stubby pencil right up to when he was about to speak. Martin Luther King's 'I Have a

Dream' speech was drafted many times and originally called '*Normalcy. Never Again*'. I can't see them printing that on t-shirts.

In case it seems a bit daunting I just want to remind you that storytelling is hardwired into us. Your children know how to do this. So did you when you were a kid. (I am assuming you were one once). Without any difficulty or training, children at play can spin stories out of nothing for hours. 'You be a dragon and I'll be Princess Leia and then the space donkey comes and we jump on his back and go to the shopping centre to fight the alien.' OK, surreal but they don't need qualifications in story construction to get going.

I'll share some finesse with you but please remember – at a basic level – you know how to do this.

And to prove it, take a look at the story below. Imagine you are telling this to an eight-year-old at bed time. He/she is an eight-year-old with a favourite toy or imaginary friend called Binky.

Binky wanted to do great things. So he did. The End.

Hmmm. That's not going to go down well with the eight-year-old. So, using the numbered lines, write five things you could do to improve the story. And boy, it could do with improving:

1. _____

2. _____

3. _____

4. _____

5. _____

If I took an educated guess I'd say you've written at least three of the following:

- Say who or what Binky is
- Describe specifically what great things she/he wanted to achieve
- And why
- Describe what was getting in the way of him/her achieving the goal
- Explain what Binky had to do to overcome those things – who or what is in the way
- Tell what happens at the end – who wins, who loses – and what is the consequence

Any eight-year-old could tell you that. So too could the eight-year-old that's still inside you – if you listened to them.

The problem is we don't. When we enter professional life we seem to put aside the storytelling ability of the playground and concentrate on the grown up business of plans.

It's great to be looking to improve your skill but do remember you've known the basic skills all your life. Stories are hardwired into us. If we're going on a journey into story, bring your inner toddler with you.

How to plan your story

Great storytelling often seems to be completely spontaneous – appearing to unfold from the speaker or writer in the moment. It isn't. Storytelling is planned. And great storytelling has a plan but you're never aware of it.

But – and it's a big 'but' – STORIES ARE NOT PLANS. If you get nothing else from this book, these four simple words can revolutionise your storytelling as a leader.

It is so important to remember because businesses and organisations, working life in general, thrive on plans. Right now intricate plans are being presented, discussed, re-discussed, re-presented in offices all over the globe. Planning is a major lever on the dashboard of business. Understandably so, at a time when everyone is seeking to figure out what comes next.

And that brings us to the first problem. The speed the world is changing and the complexity that's unfolding means that plans, while essential, are insufficient. In a world that is 'getting better and better and worse and worse, faster and faster' as my friend Jim Garrison neatly puts it, the future has arrived before your plan for it is complete.

A client who had worked for a major technology company that shall remain nameless (but, shhh, is Microsoft) tells about a planning committee for an urgently needed new building that was still meeting after the new building was built, fitted-out and occupied. For the first time in our history, the world is running faster than we can plan for. Or, as Woody Allen puts it: 'If you want to make God laugh, tell Him about your plans'.

And here's the second problem for leaders. Plans may be entertaining for 'the gods' but they are just the opposite for the people you are trying to engage.

When was the last time you turned to your loved one and said, *'Keep Thursday evening free, darling, I am taking you to town to watch a plan. It's a brand new plan, in 27 slides with pie charts and two scattergrams. You'll love it!'* Hopefully – for the health of your relationship – this is something you have never suggested. Plans are a necessary adjunct of working life, but we don't want to spend any more time than is necessary poring over them. Substitute 'latest Hollywood blockbuster' for 'plan' and Thursday night's date suddenly looks a whole lot more attractive.

Which is odd, when you think of it. Why do we spend billions of dollars a year watching, reading, enjoying stories? Especially as, when you think about it, most of these stories involve difficulty, hardship, pain, challenge, heartbreak, darkness, conflict, stress, loss and despair.

More about that later, but for now, you need to be clear about what makes a story different from a plan. This will help you as a leader better understand why your audiences find one massively more engaging than the other.

Plans v Stories

So how are stories different from plans? It's something I ask audiences all over the world. Here's what they usually say (top five):

1. 'Plans are about things, stories are about people'
2. 'Plans are about facts, stories are about feelings'
3. 'Plans are dry, stories are colourful'
4. 'Plans are dull, stories are fun'
5. 'Plans are real, stories are made up'

Clearly these are not absolute differences. Plans can be about people, and stories about things. Plans can be full of feelings (just try talking about redundancy or bonus plans and you'll see). Stories are by no means always fun. But let's not split hairs.

Your audience knows the difference between plans and stories – and while they see the merit of planning, they yearn for stories. Especially about the future.

As a leader, it's vital you remember this. Every time your audience wants a story from you and you give them a plan, you lose them.

Before we look at some simple formats for planning the stories you tell, I want to look at a few less obvious differences between plans and narratives.

Expertise v Exploration

Plans are the tool of the expert. They are designed to show you know what you are talking about. You are a master of cause and effect. If you do X then Y will follow. If that is how you are using plans, careful! It's very unlikely life is going to follow your orders. Remember those laughing gods. Stories, on the other hand, are more about what's possible than what's probable. They are a tool for exploring possibilities. We could do A or B or C. And adjust accordingly. In a world of accelerating change and complexity, do you really want to be the one saying this is exactly what is going to happen? And is that really what they want of you? Do your people look at you as a tour guide, taking them on a well-worn tourist route to the future? Or as a leader taking them on an adventure? If you don't know, ask them.

Should v Could

As someone who has spent a great deal of time in the arts and in business, I have noticed that business spends most of its time talking about what 'should' happen.

Reason rules. What you are proposing is legitimate only if you can build a 'case' for it.

The arts are focused on what 'could' happen. In my experience, artists don't create because they *ought* to but because they *want* to. In the arts, creative expression rarely requires 'sign off' by HR. Yes, market forces apply and everyone has to eat. So even the Mozarts and Michelangelos and Shakespeares produced to commission and were thinking 'commercially' about what would grab their audiences' attention. But *The Marriage of Figaro*, *Sistine Chapel* and *Hamlet* don't appear because they 'should'. We have these treasures because their creators wanted to create them.

When you are thinking about your own story of the future, be sure to consider what you want to have happen – and build your narrative on that.

Wiggly v Straight

This is the third distinction I want you to be aware of. Probably the most important for a leader. And the most counter-intuitive for anyone working in or leading an organisation.

- Plans get you from A to B by the most direct route.
- Stories get you from A to B by the most interesting route.

Plans are about efficiency. How can we traverse gaps

between where we are and where we need to go with the minimum deviation, friction, cost and at the maximum speed? Plans are about optimisation.

Imagine if we applied these criteria to a story. Romeo would meet Juliet in the first scene. And marry her happily in the third. All you'd need is a second scene where the warring Capulet and Montague families visit a mediator, bury their differences, kiss and make up. Bish, bash, bosh. A perfect plan. But a RUBBISH story. The very twists and turns that would ruin a plan are what make a tragic romance like Romeo and Juliet so compelling.

This is a head wrench for a lot of leaders – especially in business. If you're a CFO and you see things go way off plan, you scent a commercial problem. A film producer may possibly agree with you. But if you are writer, director or star and the story takes you off plan – into uncharted territory – you are more likely to scent an opportunity. It is precisely the deviation from the norm that makes the story compelling, that grabs the audience's attention, that gets us all wondering, in delicious tension, 'how are they going to get out of THAT!'

Stories are fuelled by dissonance – by things *not* being as they should be.

If stories were plans, Noah would have bought a raincoat, not built an ark. Harry would have proposed to Sally on day one. Red Riding Hood would have heeded her mother's advice and stayed home. In the professionally-

73

planned world, Pinocchio is content to be a puppet, Arthur left that sword safely in the stone and Cinderella is running a domestic cleaning agency.

Put simply, in stories, *problems are not a problem, they are an asset.*

Or, in John le Carré's words:

The cat sat on the mat is not a story.
The cat sat on the DOG's mat is a story.

Planning your story

Now there's no danger of confusing plans and stories, let's look at a few simple planning frameworks that will help you as a leader construct much better stories.

There are acres of books out there and endless academic tracts about the structure of narrative. I suggest a few below. But here I am going to wildly oversimplify because I want you to have something practical you will remember and use at work next Wednesday morning.

Essentially, all stories look a bit like this:

We start at point A. And we travel via a wiggly line (remember) to end at point B.

Point A can be thought of as the world as we know it, the status quo. It's our starting point. Point B can be thought of as the world slightly changed, a new status quo. It's our finishing point. And the line between, the meat of the story, is the sequence of events that got us from start to finish.

The wandering can be literal. There are endless myths where heroes traverse the world to complete their mission. Hercules, Odysseus, Jason, Orpheus and so on. But the wiggly line doesn't have to be a literal journey. It can be an emotional or psychological one. Love stories are good examples where two (or more) protagonists wander in and out of affection, where the obstacles are just as likely to be social as physical, where the final destination is romantic rather than geographical. Because the story voyage is internal, lovers can meet, lose and re-find each other without leaving the same apartment, railway carriage or park bench.

What this three part – or three act if you want to be arty – structure forces you to do is have…

A beginning   A   middle   An   end.

If this seems obvious – or old hat – ask yourself how often in a normal working day you bring that simple elegance to your communications or presentations. When you stand up in a meeting are you clear about where you are starting and intending to finish – and the rich filling in between? And what about the meetings themselves? How many of them follow the smooth arc from powerful beginning, via engaging journey, to a satisfying end?

Hmmm. That's what I thought.

We don't have time here to go down the meetings rabbit hole, but if you want to bring real artfulness to your meetings, I'd warmly welcome you to check out my book: *Will There Be Donuts?: How to revolutionise your business one meeting at a time.*

So, as a leader creating a narrative you want to be thinking...

- Where do I want to begin?
- Where do I want to end?
- What's the most interesting/engaging way to get there?

Careful, this is where the planner you have trained to be, could kick in, creating a nice straight line from A to B. Efficient, yes, but also really boring.

The artist Paul Klee described drawing as 'taking a line for a walk'. You could say the same for story – particularly this errant line from A to B. Take your narrative for a wander, not a route march.

Wandering isn't easy. Especially if you have been through the wander-removing process we call modern education. So to prevent getting stuck in ruler-straight A to B predictability, writers have created simple structures or spines to ensure the storyline gets good and ruffled.

Pixar, the multiple Oscar winning animation studio, should know a thing or two about constructing a compelling story. They claim their stories are all built on the following, simple spine:

1. Once upon a time there was ___.
2. Every day, ___.
3. One day ___.
4. Because of that, ___.
5. Because of that, ___.
6. Until finally ___.

Steps 1 and 2 are your beginning. Step 3 (one day) is a sign that something's changing, the journey is beginning. Story aficionados and followers of the great Joseph Campbell refer to this as the 'inciting incident'. Something happens – one day – to change the routine and upset the status quo. Steps 4 and 5 are really describing the wobbly line, the sequence of (usually unpredictable) ups and downs that lead us (finally) to step 6 and the story's conclusion.

Talking of Campbell, you can't discuss story without including his defining work on the subject, *The Hero with a Thousand Faces*. An expert in world mythology, Campbell went looking for common elements in the stories we have been telling ourselves since the dawn of civilization. In the book he distils these into a common, unifying framework – a monomyth – that he called 'The Hero's Journey'.

This is the age-old tale of the hero who is called to leave the routines of daily life and go on a perilous journey from which he or she returns bearing knowledge and/or treasure. There are many sub-steps in this tale – the call to adventure, crossing the threshold, meeting the nemesis, the lowest point, the supreme ordeal and so on. But in essence, it's the beginning-middle-end – made much richer, more powerful and meaningful.

Campbell identified 17 basic stages of the journey from the ordinary world into the special and back again.[1] People most often refer to 12 of these:

1. The Ordinary World
2. The Call to Adventure
3. Refusal of the Call
4. Meeting with the Mentor
5. Crossing the Threshold
6. Tests, Allies and Enemies

---

[1] A century before Campbell, the German novelist Gustav Freytag spotted similar way points in stories starting with *Exposition* and *Inciting Incident* then climbing through *Rising Action* to *Climax* followed by *Falling Action* down to *Resolution* and *Denouement*; a seven point plan that's become known as Freytag's Pyramid.

Academics and creative writing teachers love The Hero's Journey. It appeals to those who like puzzle breaking, symbol hunting and generally ruining the watching of movies by calling out the story signposts in advance!

I confess I love Campbell's work too. Not just the story structure but also his understanding on why myths are so important – and so needed today. It has informed much of my own writing and teaching. We'll get familiar with elements of it as we go through this short book. What I wouldn't do is recommend it as the starting point for a leader's own story making. It's a bit complex and rich for daily use. Also, I find it tends to promote a rather distorted view of the hero as a lone (male) individual who succeeds through their own efforts. We'll look more at what a hero is and isn't a bit later. For now, what I'd recommend is something a lot simpler to make sure when you are creating a narrative, you're not running through a plan.

My format is based on just two words: BUT and SO.

Imagine the elements of a plan are linked together by the word THEN.

We are here at point A. To get to point B we do this,

THEN we do this, THEN we do this, THEN we do this, THEN we do this, THEN we do this, THEN we do this and THEN we arrive at point B.

The power of story, remember, is the disruption of expectation and coping with unforeseen challenges (the cat on the dog's mat…). Here's the plan above turned into a story.

We are here at point A. To get to point B we need to do this. BUT that is going to happen SO we'll do this. BUT that could cause a backlash SO let's anticipate that. Half way through the year we'll be on track BUT remember the competition is going to be snapping at our heels SO we need to be smarter, faster and braver. We are going to get to point B BUT it's going to be hard SO let's all dig deep and get ready.

You see how the constant interruptions force you – the storyteller – to keep being creative? You see how it's more compelling, more personal, more real to be candid about the likely BUTS and not just steamroller over them with a succession of dull THEN, THEN, THEN?

You can try this with your own life story.

List what happened in the last ten years joined with a succession of thens.

[Ten years ago] I was…
then…
then…
then…

then…
then…
then…
then…
then…
until today

It's going to sound like a CV. Factual but hardly engaging.

Now try again. This time with BUT and SO.

[Ten years ago] I was…
but then…
so then…
but then…
so then…
but then…
so then…
until today

Notice how this puts energy into a series of events. The route to the here and now is interesting. Not everything went to plan. You responded to the unforeseen. You zigged. You zagged. You've had ups and downs. Your storyline is full of interest. You're a human!

OK, now you have a workable story framework, let's figure out what you need to put into it…

SEVEN STORY
MUST-HAVES

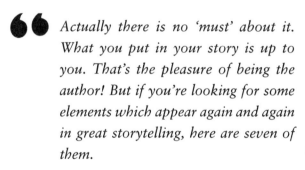 *Actually there is no 'must' about it. What you put in your story is up to you. That's the pleasure of being the author! But if you're looking for some elements which appear again and again in great storytelling, here are seven of them.*

Chapter 4

SEVEN STORY MUST-HAVES

Seven is a great storytelling number.[1] It works for Dwarves. Samurai. Brothers. And Brides for them. Even Deadly Sins. In this great tradition I am now going to offer you (drum roll) The Seven Mighty Must-Haves of Great Storytelling.

I don't want to be prescriptive here. Far too much of

---

[1] An odd number of characters is often better for storytelling than even. There is something inherently unstable about odd numbers – and, as we now know, dissonance is the fuel of interesting stories. I find this whenever my improv company takes the stage. When we are even numbered the story we make up tends to fit into comfortable pairings. And while couples can be dramatic, there's nothing like an odd one out – man or women – to heat up the temperature and force change onto the stage.

that these days in personal and professional life. The joy of storytelling is, of course, that you can include whatever the heck you like. Unlike school homework, or college exams, or job applications, or business plans, or engagement proposals, or monthly reports, or tax returns… or any of the growing number of rule-bound forms we have to fill in. Take the freedom that storytelling offers you and include material you wouldn't normally in your leadership communication.

But here are seven elements which will definitely add dynamism and sticking power to your storytelling. Use the ones which are most useful.

Must-have #1: A hero

To go on a hero's journey you are going to need a hero. But let's be clear from the start what we *don't* mean by 'hero'.

A hero isn't necessarily…

… a man

I say this because there is such a bias towards men in hero roles it's easy to start thinking it's a masculine role. A woman delegate grabbed me after one talk on the hero's journey and complained about the unconscious gender bias in the term: 'Hero has the word HE in it!' I did point out it also has the word H-E-R in it, but I totally take the point. Hero and heroine should be totally interchangeable. Or, like the word 'actor', hero should be assumed to be gender free.

… a human

E.T. Flipper. Wall-E. Champion the Wonder Horse. Mickey Mouse. Pinocchio. Jonathan Livingstone Seagull. The Hobbit. Nemo. Woody. Spongebob Squarepants. OK, maybe Spongebob is humanoid, but I rest my case. If you're a storyteller, anyone or anything can be a hero.

… an individual

Stories abound with a group hero, where multiple characters collectively take on the hero role. Think films. Those seven Samurai, for a start. And Platoon. The Right Stuff. The Godfather. Oceans 11 to 31… All ensemble performances. This is particularly important to remember if you are going to be storytelling in a culture that favours collaboration over individual heroics. It's why I often rewrite hero's journey as *heroes' journey*.

A hero is not even necessarily *heroic*. In fact, outside the two-dimensional storytelling of superhero comics, heroes rarely are conventionally heroic. You know, the type that laughs in the face of danger, feels no fear and catches bullets in their teeth. The heroes you need to focus on – and which your audiences will connect with – are *ordinary people who do extraordinary things*.

A more technical, but less emotionally loaded way to describe the hero of the story is the *protagonist* – derived from Greek drama meaning literally 'first actor or main character'. Another no-nonsense definition of protagonist that I like, from the theatre director Peta Lily, is: 'The person in the story to whom most happens'.

In your story that's you!

This is something worth dwelling on. You are the hero of your story. When I tell audiences, particularly corporate, professional audiences this, they usually give me a disbelieving look as if to say 'who – us?' They don't usually think of themselves as living a story. And they certainly don't feel heroic (as in courageous, selfless, visionary, persistent and downright Mandela-like). Of course they don't. I doubt Mandela felt Mandela-like. Indeed, I heard a story while in South Africa – from someone who knew him well – which shows how lightly Madiba held his own hero status.

My friend was part of a group of young leaders visiting a psychiatric hospital in Durban. While the visitors checked in, Mandela wandered off and, as was his style, fell into conversation with an inmate sitting on a bench. After a couple of minutes Mandela roared with laughter and returned to the group explaining:

> *The gentlemen over there asked me who I was and I said, 'Nelson Mandela.' The inmate patted me kindly on the arm and said comfortingly, 'They all say that when they arrive. It'll pass.'*

Very few of us look into the bathroom mirror in the morning and see a hero staring back at them. Sure, there are days when we feel superhuman but – it passes. So what qualifies you to be the hero of your story? What characteristic DO you share with the heroes of myth and legend?

I've read my fair share of stories and I would say there's one quality all heroes have. Without it there would be no story. It's not epic – it's ordinary. And you've felt it many times this week already. You might even be feeling it right now. In fact the longer I go on with this sentence the more you are going to be feeling it.

It is Frustration. Frustration is a sign that the world around you isn't acting as you think it should. Or – and this is very important for heroes – that you are not behaving as the world around you thinks you should.

Remember the status quo I mentioned. Point A where the story starts. Well the thing about the hero is they don't quite fit the status quo. There's something about who they are, how they think, what they want that makes them a misfit in the world around them.

It could be they are truly a misfit – an ugly duckling in a tribe of swans. Or just that they see the world differently – a Jonathan Livingstone Seagull that wants to push the envelope of flight. Maybe they just ask the questions others don't, like: 'What's in the woods?' And when people tell them, 'we don't go into the woods,' they break the taboo and head off into the undergrowth to find out.

It's what I think of as The Protagonist's Itch. The nagging voice that says:

'There's a bigger world out there…'

'There has to be a better way…'

'I am better than this…'

'I can see something that no-one else can…'

'Somewhere, over the rainbow, skies are blue…'

If you look at the stories – including real life stories – where anything exceptional is achieved, you will find a protagonist with an itch right at the middle of it. Every world-changing invention. Every speed record broken. Every disruptive start-up. Every social innovation and human rights advance. Every awe-inspiring edifice. They all happened because someone questioned the status quo – and when people said *you can go only this far…* they went further.

My accountant, Lawrence, uses The Protagonist's Itch as a way of screening time-wasting clients. If someone comes to him claiming they want to make a significant change in their business he presents them with what he calls the Change Formula.

$$V \times P \times D = C$$

Try it yourself. Think of something significant you want to change in your life and/or business. Score yourself out of ten in each of the first three values. C is the likelihood you will actually make the change you say you want to make. You need to score 700/1000 or over for my accountant to take you on. V stands for Vision. And P for Plan. But what is D?

Determination? Desire? Decision? Drive?

All useful, but the critical factor – according not only to my financial advisor but also generations of story-tellers – is...

DISCONTENT

That's right. You can have all the plans in the world. And the most technicolour vision of where you'd like to be. But unless you are sufficiently discontent, frustrated, itchy about how things are, you are never going to move.

This frustration is the engine of story. If you look closely, it's also the engine of enterprise.

As a leader you would do well to identify the frustrations in yourself, your team, your organisation. And harness it in your storytelling!

There is a deeper reason the protagonist gets itchy. That's because, whether they know it or not, they have a motivation, a mission, a want, a why.

Must-have #2: A why

Why did Romeo and Juliet have to die, Daddy? My ten-year-old daughter was asking this through her tears. She was more sobbing than asking actually. And it was my fault. I had thought it was time to introduce her to some Shakespeare and reckoned *Romeo and Juliet* would do the trick. Nice one, Dad! She had been fine at the start of the performance, then concerned, alarmed, shocked and, finally, inconsolable. I explained it was just a story, that these were just actors, that the poison was Ribena and the knife was made of rubber, but it was no use. Elsa wanted an answer. And it's a question all good storytelling forces us to ask.

Storytelling, remember, is one of humanity's oldest teaching tools. It is designed to help us understand the world and ourselves better. That means exciting our curiosity and encouraging us to ask questions.

And the most powerful of these is *why*?

Why do Juliet's parents insist she marries someone she clearly doesn't love? And *why* didn't Juliet obey them? She'd be Prince Paris's princess by now. Not happy, perhaps, but alive. *Why* does Romeo brave death to shin up the ivy to Juliet's balcony? (OK, we know why a man does that…) But *why* does he then kill her kinsman and get himself exiled? *Why* doesn't Juliet wake a moment sooner? And *why*, Dad, didn't you anticipate this torrent of *whys*?

What is important, of course. We're curious about the action. But, in truth, we can quite often guess a lot of the *what* in advance.

You're going to a romantic comedy featuring two highly paid, good looking stars with great teeth? It's no secret they are going to fall in love and be together at the end. When James Bond comes up against an actor who is carrying a wicked looking knife and a scarred face – do we really doubt who is going to end up in the dust?

In the prologue to *Romeo and Juliet*, Shakespeare actually tells us what's going to happen before we have even settled in our seats:

Two households, both alike in dignity,
In fair Verona, where we lay our scene,
From ancient grudge break to new mutiny,
Where civil blood makes civil hands unclean.
From forth the fatal loins of these two foes
A pair of star-cross'd lovers take their life;

Spoiler alert! The kids aren't coming out of this love story alive. But that doesn't in any way lessen our enjoyment. Because the events of a story – the *what* – are really only the surface.

How is also important. The puzzle-solving part of our mind is curious about the mechanics. *How* does the drama unfold? *How* does the hero win against overpowering odds when all seemed lost? *How* does an innocent love end in a double-suicide?

But while the audience is interested in *what* and *how*, they are truly fascinated by *why*.

Why reveals the deeper motivations powering the story and its characters, the intentions that make them choose option A rather than B, C or D.

As a storytelling leader you need to be aware of this and build your stories from the *why* upwards.

There are probably three main questions you should anticipate your audience is going to be asking:

1. *Why this story?*
What's the message, lesson or provocation at the heart of the story? What are you trying to get across. If it's a pointless anecdote you'll quickly lose their attention – and you deserve to.

2. *Why should they listen?*
Where's the value in this story for them? How is it relevant, interesting, informative, inspiring? Think of those ancient storytellers around the flickering fire. What nugget of wisdom are you passing on to your tribe, wrapped in an entertaining story? What questions do you want them to ask themselves when they've heard it?

3. *What's your why?*
These are skeptical times. People are hungry for authentic leadership and wary of propaganda. 'People don't buy what you do, they buy why you do it.' So says Simon Sinek, author of the global bestseller, *Start With Why*. Your audience at work isn't just listening to your story, they are watching to see if you mean it. Leaders are meaning-makers, remember. So before you tell your story, take a moment to check your deeper intention in

telling it; to inspire, inform, cajole, develop, stimulate, provoke, empower, illustrate, embolden, awaken, accelerate, focus, encourage, inspire ... you choose. If you do this, match your intention and your tale, your audience will get the double whammy of a meaningful story told by a leader who means it.

But why did Romeo and Juliet have to die, Daddy?

Elsa is still looking at me quizzically through her tears. Some whys don't have a simple answer. But, in this complex world, that's even more reason to ask them.

Must-have #3: Allies

One of the reasons I prefer the 'heroes' journey' to 'hero's' is that, when you step back and look, you see that no hero, however self-reliant, makes it through the journey alone. The journey is peppered with allies, guides, helpers and subsidiary characters without whom the protagonist would not make it.

How far would Dorothy have skipped down the yellow brick road without the Tin Man, Lion and Scarecrow? Without the Munchkins, or Glinda, Good Witch of the North or the ever-vigilant dog Toto. Given all she's up against, she'd have tripped at the first brick.

In stories, as in life, success is a group effort.

And the group doesn't just appear on cue, arranged by a helpful HR department. No, Dorothy – and her fellow protagonists down the ages – had to find and enrol them.

The first part of her journey is building the cast of allies that will enable her to complete the journey.

It's entertaining to see the squad gather or the samurai assemble, to see Danny Ocean's crew grow from 2 to 11. But there's a deeper importance to this phase of the story – which is especially relevant to today's leaders.

We're living in an age that's too complex for any one hero. It's a time of open-source creativity; as Kevin Kelly, the co-founder of WIRED magazine, puts it: 'None of us is as smart as *all* of us.'

The hero's need for allies neatly mirrors this more collaborative spirit. None of us will reach our own personal and professional Oz alone.

We all have blind spots, limits to what we know, think and can perceive. The allies provide additional perspective which the lone hero lacks. Without them we are fatally blinkered. With them we get 360, wraparound vision.

D'Artagnan has all the swash and buckle you could want from a young Musketeer. And yet it's only with the wisdom of Athos, the bravado of Porthos and the seductive charm of Aramis that this naïve young hero can beat the dastardly Comte de Rochefort and Cardinal Richelieu. There are endless romances and romantic comedies where the two lovers initially dislike each other intensely. And it's only when they realise their contrary ways of looking at the world, seeing how they complement each other and build a complete view that they then fall in love. Buddy movies are driven in a similar way. Two people with very distinct, partial views of the world, ultimately gel spectacularly in a narrative version of 1+1=5.

Even the quintessentially independent mind of Sherlock Holmes needs a dependable, feet-on-the-ground foil and sense-checker like Dr Watson at his side. Multi-disciplinary teams sound new. But the allies of world storytelling have anticipated them for centuries.

Allies, note. Not *friends*.

This is a crucial thing to remember when you are putting a story or, for that matter, a winning team, together. The protagonist needs allies around them, not *friends*.

The key difference is, I think, that friends will tell you what you want to hear. And allies, what you *need* to hear.

The adventurer Robert Swan, a loner by heart, tried to walk solo to the South Pole and failed. For his next attempt, he reluctantly pulled together the best-qualified group of specialists he could find as allies. Ten days into the expedition he was regretting his decision, stomping around in the snow, irritated by the many annoying qualities of this highly qualified but socially-awkward bunch of experts. 'Why didn't I bring my friends?' he asked himself. And then the realisation stopped him in his tracks. 'I could have brought my friends, but we would have *died*.'

Annoying though allies can be – and sometimes their

role is to annoy – it's allies you need in hostile or demanding circumstances, not friends.

The lesson for leaders is – in your storytelling (as in your real life leadership) – make sure to gather a diverse cast of allies to complement and check what the hero or heroes are up to.

Gather allies. You're going to need them. And here's why…

Must-have #4: The nemesis

'Hist!' cried Holmes, and I heard the sharp click of a cocking pistol. 'Look out! It's coming!' I sprang to my feet, my inert hand grasping my pistol, my mind paralyzed by the dreadful shape, which had sprung out upon us from the shadows of the fog. A hound it was, an enormous coal-black hound, but not such a hound as mortal eyes have ever seen. (*The Hound of the Baskervilles* by Sir Arthur Conan Doyle)

You're going to need allies because we know who's out there. Beyond the comfort of the world we know. We'd rather not face them, but we can't do without them. They exhaust us, but give us the energy to go on. They go bump in the night. They lurk under the bed waiting to grab our heels. They are cloaked by mist and howl under a moonless sky. They threaten our projects, our peace of mind, our very existence.

We call them the baddies.

But there is nothing bad about them. Indeed, for you as a storytelling leader, they are quite the opposite. They're your besties.

Think of all the stories we love because of the evil character in them. Clarice Starling (Jodie Foster's character in *Silence of the Lambs*) is a great protagonist. But it's the cannibalistic Hannibal Lecter that has become a cultural meme. Luke Skywalker may have been the formal hero of Star Wars (with Hans Solo as the raffish anti-hero) but it is Darth Vader that towers over the six (and soon to be more) films of the Lucasfilm franchise.

I have personal experience of that particular character because I was him. In a fashion. For a year after university I worked for Lucasfilm, travelling up and down the country wearing the costume from the film, opening supermarkets and signing autographs. Not glamorous, but interesting. Particularly at Christmas when I would be appearing alongside Santa Claus at department stores. Who was more popular? No contest. Give an eight-year-old the choice between a jolly ho-ho-ho-ing present-bearing grandad with a white beard, and an overgrown black-caped man with a cockroach face and Nazi helmet? I won every time.

There is something about a great villain that transcends scary.

I have dwelt on this and think there are three reasons we are so drawn to villains.

99

First, at some deeper level we realise they are only the flip side of the hero coin. Good guy and bad guy are actually dancing partners. No protagonist can be great without an equally excellent antagonist. This is why, rather than baddie, I prefer the term 'nemesis' or 'worthy opponent'.

Second, they are not evil. Not in their own terms. Once we step inside their shoes we realise there is a logic to their thinking. The conflict between hero and nemesis is not usually founded on genuine hatred – though that can be a consequence. Usually it's just that the nemesis wants something or someone. And the hero stands in their way. It's not dissimilar in business. Your competitor rarely hates you or wishes you harm, at least I hope not. What they want – for perfectly valid reasons – is your market share. They want to expand and you stand in their way. You both want to acquire the same company and you will do battle to get it.

And thirdly, the baddie is YOU. How's that? When you read a story, most people identify with the main character. Whether it's fighter pilot, young wizard, eighteenth century governess, Roman Emperor or ugly duckling – the hero is us. When we read about them, at one level we become them. We care. We hold our breath when they are in difficulties. We inwardly cheer when they make it.

As a leader it is worth remembering, for your people, the nemesis very often is you. It's you that initiates routine-disturbing change. You are the one with the vision that requires them to stir themselves to action. You are the one wanting more for the team or business than it wants for itself. You are the one who has new ideas that upset their world, turning things upside down by reading books like this one.

But empathy doesn't stop there. I would say we actually identify with every character of the story; the smaller helper characters, the cameo parts, the love interest and – yes – the nemesis. Anyone whose feelings and thoughts we can imagine. Put more simply, every character in a story is us. Indeed if you trace drama back to its roots in the temples of ancient Greece, that was its function. Drama was invented so that humans could sit in the dark and watch the better and worse parts of themselves fight it out on stage while we watched in comfort in the dark. It was a form of vicarious conflict resolution. If you could watch terrible things on stage, they were less likely to manifest in life. Every war enacted was one less actually fought. As my drama teacher at Cambridge once said, drama is like being 'tickled by a dagger'. Terror turned titillation.

So, storytelling leaders, if your tales lack power, find a more compelling nemesis. Or beef up the one you have.

I have lost count of the number of times I have heard leaders seek to create confidence by minimising difficulty. The result is the exact opposite of what they intend. Yes, you want to radiate confidence – but don't minimise the potential threat of what you are up against. If you want to improve people's performance, create a worthy adversary for them to face.

No-one raises their game for a 'push-over'. It's the Hound of the Baskervilles, remember. Hound. Not puppy.

Must-have #5: Highs and lows

After a storytelling workshop in India, a young woman delegate stopped me and asked for a word. She was worried about the timeline she'd drawn in the session. It was a diagonal line rising without a bump from the bottom left of the page to the top right. Her concern was that she'd done the exercise wrong and that her lifeline shouldn't look that way. My advice to her as a student was to look closer at her life and just check she wasn't editing the inevitable ups and downs out. My advice to her as a writer would have been – yes WORRY! Worry a lot. Diagonally rising lines are death to stories. Straight ones of any direction are. Who wants to hear a story which keeps travelling remorselessly in the same direction – be it up or down? Stories need highs and, even more importantly, lows.

Here are two great things to know about highs:

1. Highs can't last

The most important thing to know about a high in a story is – it is *temporary*. It's like a tennis ball you have thrown up into the sky and is hanging there at the zenith of its flight – about to fall down again. In stories – as in life – highs are transitory. And thank heaven they are. Imagine an existence that was uninterruptedly, ecstatically 'high'. At best, the high would become the new norm. At worst, bliss would turn to hell.

It's worth saying this because all around us, every day, the opposite message is being pushed on us. The underlying message of many – actually I'd say most – advertising campaigns is: *Buy this and your troubles are over. Forever.*

The beguiling beach holiday shot. The healthy septuagenarian couple enjoying life aboard their yacht thanks to their insurance company. Even the new cleaner that will massacre all household germs. Each is selling you a release from the ups and downs of daily life. They all promise an end to strife and struggle. Finally you will look good, feel good, be loved, have great breath/health/sex. Our humdrum life will be transformed into adventure, the traffic-crammed city street into a deserted highway with just us on it – top down, racing noiselessly, leaving all our cares behind. It's the myth of OK-ness. Pleasant-ville. We knows it's fake. But we buy it every time.

As an improviser, you quickly find how uninteresting it is for things to 'work out OK.' You're in a scene and someone produces a [mimed] revolver. I used to do anything I could to stop that gun going off. Throw it offstage.

Melt it. Discover it was shooting blanks. Turn it into a cauliflower. Anything to make things 'OK'. And the audience hated it. We don't come to the theatre to see things be 'OK'. We have our lives for that. It's nice when stories work out. But that's not why we're listening.

As a storyteller you have to understand that the audience is cruel. They want the opposite of the careful performer. They want to see blood. They want to see you put the imaginary gun to the main character's head and blow their imaginary brains all over the back wall. And then to see how you'll get out of the horrible problem you have just caused for yourself.

If in doubt, watch a group of toddlers shooting, skewering, eviscerating each other in an average playground.

High points are great but they kill the story stone dead if they go on too long. The story can end on a high, sure. But the words 'and they lived happily ever after' are like a bell tolling to let us know the story we enjoyed is now dead and gone forever. For our inner eight-year-old it also means *lights out, it's time for bed*. No wonder we hate it.

So enjoy the high but don't dwell on it.

No, the great thing about the high is that it teasingly awakens us to what's coming next – the LOW.

2. Highs make us stupid

There is a reason highs are followed by lows. And usually it's because highs make us happy. And happy people are less awake.

Leaders beware.

As Bill Gates puts it:

Success is a lousy teacher. It seduces smart people into thinking they can't fail.

On the day of their investiture, the Emperors of Rome would employ an advisor to ride with them in their triumphal chariot, whispering 'remember you are mortal'. They knew that at the highest points, humans are most prone to god-like self-delusion. It is the sin of 'hubris' which dictates when we fly closest to the sun, we are most likely to melt our wings and find ourselves hurtling back to earth with the aerodynamics of a set of car keys.

Storytellers know this and use this reversal of fortune to great effect. For example, there is usually a moment somewhere about a third of the way through a story where the hero gets what they have been asking for and discovers it's a far harder problem than they had ever anticipated. The what-have-I-gotten-myself-into moment. And there's another, about two thirds of the way in when the hero appears to achieve their goal only to discover a horrible truth. The goal was misguided or the actual end point is in another direction. Or the person they most relied on as a friend turns out to be an enemy. We love these reversals. Aristotle, when he was teaching story, called it *peripeteia* – the moment when the protagonist's fortunes turn from good to bad – and insisted his students included it in their narratives.

Leaders know that a really good story goes down as well as up – that the sunny uplands of Storyland are separated by deep, dark valleys. And they are not there just as an obstacle – an occupational hazard.

Here are two great things to know about the lows:

1. Lows make us smarter

Think about your own story line. When did you learn the most? When everything was going swimmingly. Or when you were really up against it? Characters don't end up in low points by accident. They are driven there by what they don't know – by their blind spots. Good storytellers drive their characters there so that they can learn something. Usually something they have been ignoring…

… or forgetting…

… or…denying.

If I look back into my own story, there was a time – it seems like another life now – when I was fighting depression. And even harder, fighting the idea I even had depression. 'Oh, I'm fine', I told myself, 'it's the rest of the world that's gone mad.' Things got progressively bleaker until one day I was sitting in the twilight on a park bench in Cambridge and I noticed a group of really bedraggled homeless men approaching me. I felt a bit scared and mostly embarrassed as I didn't have any cash to give them. But it wasn't my help they wanted. As it turned out they wanted to help me. 'Are you OK, mate?' they asked. 'Come with us, we'll find you somewhere to stay'. It was touching but deeply shocking too. These desperate people had seen through my act and recognised someone equally desperate. It jolted me out of my self-deception and, though I didn't accept their offer of accommodation, I did seek some professional help. And depression is now a distant memory. For me, at least.

This kind of jolt is one of the most satisfying points in story (and in life); a turning point. It's the moment when a plunging storyline shifts direction and nudges upwards. All the downward energy is converted into narrative 'lift.' Certainly for me, that *de*pression was also *com*pression – like loading energy into a spring – it produces an equal and opposite bounce.

2. Lows engage your listener

Humans don't huddle in the dark and invest their time listening to tales about people whose lives work perfectly. We want to know the protagonist is like us. Flawed.

One of the very earliest stories ever recorded is called *Trickster Burns His Ass*. It's not a sophisticated tale. The title tells you all you need to know. Trickster, the quintessential human everyman, thinks he can sit on a fire without burning his bottom. He is wrong. If you listen hard you can hear the chortling of our ancestors enjoying this simple tale. Delighting in the fact that the hapless hero is just like us.

People mess up. We all mess up. In the professional world messing up is something people tend to hide. As an author you shout it from the rooftops because it builds a bridge of empathy with your audience.

The lesson for you as a leader? If you want to impress people, tell them your achievements, your high point. If you want to *lead* them, share your difficulties, your lows and how you dealt with them. Which brings us to must-have numero 6…

Must-have #6: Choices, choices

When I was eight, I sang at the Royal Opera House. I sang there for four years, actually. All the boy soprano parts. It's a long story and one probably best told another time. The roles I sang were usually short and involved me hanging around a lot backstage. So I watched. And listened. And fell in love.

Loving opera wasn't a popular choice for a schoolboy. I got to skip exams two years in a row – but for six months my hair was shaped into a ridiculous page-boy style. Even today, opera is hardly hip.

The standard criticism people throw at opera – apart from the seat prices – is 'the stories are dumb'. They're right. And wrong.

If you judge a story purely by the actions in it, opera's do sound ridiculously far-fetched. Take *Tosca*, an opera I sang over 70 times when I was a kid. Here's a summary of the action:

An opera singer (Floria Tosca) loves a painter (Mario Cavaradossi) who is secretly a revolutionary activist. The police chief Scarpia loves Tosca and – long and short of it – gets the painter slung in jail and will only free him if he can have his wicked way with her. She appears to agree but once she has the pardon in her hand, stabs Scarpia with a fruit knife.

OK so far? I warn you it doesn't end well.

Floria goes to the prison to spring her lover. But it turns out Scarpia has double crossed her from his grave. A mock execution turns into a real execution. And when Tosca discovers Mario is dead, kills herself rather than be arrested for Scarpia's murder.

So that's the action. And I agree, it may not leap off the page for a 21st century reader. But here's the thing you need to know about stories – operatic and otherwise. It's not the action that we're really interested in. It's the choices the characters make.

I'll say that again. Not actions. But choices.

Action movies may entertain for an evening, but won't last a lifetime. Years later, I don't remember those performances of Tosca I watched from the wings because of what the character did. But the choices she has to make.

And they are agonising. The middle act is set in the police chief's apartment. It's a seduction scene with a cruel twist. Under the floor is a detention cell where Scarpia is torturing Floria's lover for information about the whereabouts of a revolutionary friend. Scarpia knows Tosca has the secret information and presents her with a cruel choice. She can stay loyal to her lover and hear him die. Or betray his trust and spare him. By fessing up, she is confirming the painter's guilt and possibly signing his death warrant. But if she doesn't, she will be responsible for him dying on the rack.

An agonising choice, right?

And we love it. We love seeing someone else in a terrible situation while we sit in comfort in the dark. We love second-guessing what she will do, and wondering what we would do in the same situation. And we love it because Puccini lavishes amazing music to illustrate the emotional trauma – pages of it. The tenor moans in pain. The baritone goads the soprano. The soprano soars in indecision, begging for respite, for mercy.

Basic storytelling communicates the action. Opera, film, all great storytelling dwells in the choices, the spaces between the action.

Tosca's torment – and our empathetic enjoyment of it – isn't over. Later in the scene, with no choice but to sleep with her tormentor, Tosca spots the knife Scarpia has been using to peel his dessert. She doesn't do anything. She just looks at the knife, and the suspenseful music throws us back in the world of choices. What is she going to do? Murder Scarpia or sleep with him? Kiss or kill? And when you decide to kill your enemy – can you physically or morally do it?

Turns out she can, by the way. Kill him. And stand over him as he suffocates in his own blood. But then, before she sweeps off to prison and her own date with death, she makes a touchingly unexpected choice. She places two candles at the head of the corpse of her mortal enemy and sings:

Or gli perdono!

Now, I pardon him!

It's not the killing that involves us. We can see that in any video game any day of the week. In true storytelling, what hooks us are the choices that lead up to and follow it.

Super heroes just act. Real heroes choose to act.

We are addicted to watching people make choices. And the more difficult the better.

The most difficult choices you can face, by the way, are dilemmas. How so? Because most of the time life asks us to choose between right and wrong. These decisions can be hard enough. What makes dilemmas especially demanding is the fact they force us to choose between two rights. Or two wrongs.

Authors love to do this to their heroes. Think

Sophie's Choice – a mother forced to choose which of her two children is to live and which to die. Or Faust, who was offered everything he wants in this life in return for damnation in the next. Say you wouldn't be even a little bit tempted. Or the classic, do-you-love-her-enough-to-let-her-go dilemma that Humphrey Bogart's Rick faces with the married Ilsa (Ingrid Bergman) in *Casablanca*.

Authors aren't sadists. On the contrary, they know the kindest thing they can do for a character is to put them in the teeth of an agonizing conundrum and have the audience on tenterhooks to see what choice they make. We love these characters for making the tough decisions. And we love that they are having to do this, not us.

For the leader, this is high-octane story fuel.

Must-have #7: Surprise!

- If you really want to delight your audience
- If you care for them
- If you want them to remember and love you
- If you want them to feel time spent in your presence was worth every second
- If you want them to hang onto every word
- If you want them queueing round the block and coming back for more
- If you want them purring in your hands like a giant multi-headed tabby cat

Then…

There's one thing you must do as a storyteller.
It's written on the next page.
But don't turn yet.
Guess the word.
Two syllables.
Starts with an S ends with an E.
Rhymes with French fries.
    Yes, the one thing you have to get really good at as a storyteller is [turn the page now]…

S A U S A G E

OK, I know that's not what you expected. And I lied about the French fries. But that's what this section is about.

The power of SURPRISE as an engine of storytelling.

If you want to hook your audience you will give them what they want *but not in the way they expect it*. You will not be predictable, except to lull them into a false sense of security. Which will make the surprise all the more of a jolt.

It is a mild form of torture. One that your audience doesn't just allow you to do – they expect you to do it. They will even PAY you to. It's reckoned Agatha Christie's tales of suspense and surprise have sold four billion copies. She's second only to Shakespeare on the bestsellers-of-all-time lists. That's a lot of people wanting a storyteller to flummox, misdirect and wrong foot them.

We spend most of our lives trying to make the world predictable. We go to the storyteller to be teased, tormented and titillated by the *un*predictable.

It's massively entertaining. And as a leader you would do well to remember the need not just to inform but to surprise your people.

They want you to jolt them out of their everyday thinking. They crave the frisson of the unforeseen.

They are expecting the unexpected. Do not disappoint them.

Here are a few ways to build surprise even into fairly straightforward story situations.

The misdirect

You send the audience one way and they abruptly turn the corner or the page to find they are somewhere else. See the SAUSAGE example above.

Comics do this well. In fact that's what many jokes are – a verbal misdirect.

Man walks into a bar.
Ouch!

At the very least it will get a laugh. There are volumes of scholarly analysis about what laughing is and why human beings (with the exception of some US border guards I have met) were born with a sense of humour at all. The explanation that makes most sense to me is that the laughter is a release of tension. A joke like this clashes one reality (bar as drinking place) with another (bar as lump of metal). This stresses the brain.

The brain is trying to keep you safe. And that entails keeping a close eye (and ear) on words that have a variety of different, potentially confusing meanings. How much more dangerous would the world be if we really couldn't tell the difference between a harmless drink and a head threatening lump of metal? If *whole* was confused with a *hole*. If we couldn't distinguish illness (ail) and beer (ale). If you mistakenly put your life savings in a bank (of a river) not a bank (on the high street).

The joke teller's pun violates this rule and causes a micro-moment of distress for the disorientated brain. When we realise it's not a life-threatening one we release the tension in a laugh.

It's not only a great technique for entertaining your people, it can be very helpful for a leader who wants to get the audience to break a thinking habit and look at life a little differently.[2] Take this riddle-like tale:

> *A boy is being driven to school by his dad when their car is hit by another. The boy is badly hurt in the accident and his father is killed. The ambulance arrives and speeds the boy to hospital. When he arrives the doctor opens the ambulance door and says 'This is my son.' How come?*

The surprise is – of course – that the doctor is the boy's mother. I say, of course, but you'd be amazed by the time

---

[2] ... and getting people to buy things. It has been shown recently [Derick F. Davis and Paul M. Herr, *Journal of Consumer Research*, April 2014] that using sound-alike words 'primes' people to purchase. So, for example, saying 'bye' or 'goodbye' predisposes people to *buy* or think they are getting a *good buy*.

it takes for some groups to get the answer. Female groups included! The word doctor – culturally weighted in favour of males – is a misdirect. A cultural misdirect. You can use stories like this to surprise people into recognising their habitual thinking and unconscious biases.

Broken promise

This is a counter-intuitive technique which I have discovered works well, particularly with impatient listeners. You promise to give them some crucial piece of information: 'I'll tell you more about that in a moment...' And then you *don't* give it. Somewhere deep in the neural cortex, the audience is hooked, hungry for that final piece of data. Whether they realise it or not, they start concentrating more.

Try this by saying at the start of the meeting, 'I am going to ask you an important question in a minute or two...' Keep referring to the question but don't actually ask it. When you do finally ask it, at the end of the meeting, you're closing an annoyingly open circuit in the listener's mind and, unconsciously, they will thank you for that. And there's a good chance they will actually answer the question you are posing.

The reveal

'Luke, I am your father...' The moment we learn Darth Vader's true identity is possibly the best known unmasking in modern storytelling. Granted anyone with a smattering of German would have guessed that anyone named Vader was likely to be someone's Father (Vater). But that aside, it's an example of the time-honoured storytelling technique – called *anagnorisis*, or discovery, by Aristotle – where a character turns out not to be who you thought they were.

The most famous in Greek tragedy is when Oedipus discovers that he has not only killed his father but that the woman he married is – awkward – his mother.

I wouldn't suggest you go this far in your own storytelling. But, I'd certainly have a go at putting a surprise *reveal* in your narrative – if only to enjoy the gratifying 'aha' effect this causes in your audience.

For instance, there's a story I like to tell to companies who want to innovate but are unwilling to make mistakes.

It concerns three men and a pigeon. It's 1964. Two boffins in New Jersey decide to map the Milky Way and build a super sensitive radio telescope to do this. The only problem is, it's too sensitive. Try as they may they cannot get rid of an annoying background static that is clouding their readings. They think it's interference from New York City but when they point the telescope at Manhattan the signal does not increase. They think it's the fallout from a recent nuclear bomb test but the buzz remains even when the fallout dissipates. They finally think it may be a pigeon who has nested in the telescope and left a digestive contribution to the experiment in the scope. But having climbed into the telescope and hand scrubbed the 'white dielectric material' away, there was still no improvement. They persisted for a year, trying to mute the sound with aluminium tape and scratching their heads. It seemed their telescope was a failure. At their wits' end they picked up the phone and spoke to a nuclear physicist they knew in Princeton to see if he could fix their technical problem. Bob listened as they described their troubles and then groaned. 'You scooped us!' Bob, you see, had spent years searching for that annoying hum – which turned out not to be a disturbance at all but residual radiation left over from the genesis of the world, proof that the Big Bang actually happened!

At this point I reveal that the two boffins are Robert Wilson and Arno Penzias of Bell Labs. Bob, is Robert Dicke at Princeton. And their technical failure turned out to be a world-changing breakthrough, earning them each a Nobel Prize.

Spoiler alert!

I can't leave the subject of 'reveals' without sharing what I think are two of the best surprises in cinema. If you haven't seen these films yourself, look away now.

In *The Sixth Sense*, the 1999 film by M. Night Shyamalan, the main character (played by Bruce Willis) has spent the whole film helping a boy communicate with the dead. It is only at the end he discovers he himself is – DEAD.

My other personal favourite is *Fight Club* where the narrator, played by Edward Norton, discovers that Tyler Durden (Brad Pitt), his side-kick throughout the movie, doesn't actually exist but is just one of his own multiple personalities.

Deus-ex-machina

The dramatists of ancient Greece loved getting their characters in an almighty pickle and then having the gods appear from heaven to sort it all out. The Gods were literally craned in on a theatrical winch, hence the expression *Deus ex Machina* or 'god from the machinery'. The fairy godmother is our modern equivalent.

In storytelling terms it's the surprise resolution of a problem by unexpected or even improbable means.

Steve Jobs was a leader who used this technique frequently in his famous product launches. He'd set the context, describe the problem, identify the customer need and then whip out the iPhone or iPad – like a heavenly answer to everyone's prayers.

Closer to home, there was a story my dad used to tell – against himself as it happens – which uses the device perfectly.

My dad, Bernard Pearl, was a huge lover of life. And a hater of hotels. Truth be told, he never really wanted to stay anywhere but his own house. And hotel managers throughout the known world bore the brunt of his irritation about being away.

My mother knew this and would never unpack in the first room they were assigned. She'd sit patiently while my dad would test the bed (too squishy), the pillow (too hard), the view (no sea view), the distance from door to lift (too far to roll cases, too close to sleep without hearing the 'ding'), the fruit bowl (not sufficiently cornucopia alike). She knew he'd then storm off to 'have words' with the manager. He'd usually do these at full volume in the most prominent part of the lobby. 'They always want you to step into their office' he counselled me once. 'Don't! The more noise you make in public, the quicker they'll cave in.' These words could result in them leaving the room, the hotel, or even the city.

Until one day, in the USA, my dad met his match.

My parents had flown to Boston, Massachusetts, for a week of sightseeing. They checked into a quaint townhouse boutique hotel. And the normal checklist began. My dad stormed into the lobby, whacked the concierge bell and called for the manager. Out came a smiling young man in a polyester suit with beige piping named – according to his badge – Dwayne. 'Are you the manager?' my dad seethed and started to vent his room-rage. But Dwayne cut him off with a smile and a question. 'What room did they give you, Mr Pearl?' My dad held up the key (an old fashioned one with tag) and waved it in front of Dwayne's face. '306!'

Dwayne's face fell: '306? You are right, Mr Pearl. The bed is too squishy, the pillows are like rock, you indeed cannot see the sea, the fruit bowl is woeful and no-one could sleep that close to the lift. Here…'

He turned to the key rack behind the reception desk, fished out six keys and plonked them in front of my father.

'… Mr Pearl, go find yourself a room.'

A genius piece of customer service from someone who knew no-one could please my dad better than my dad. But also a great climax to a story. Not so much a sting-in-the-tail as a taking-the-wind-out-of-your-sails. It isn't only my dad who is taken by surprise, the listener is too.

For the record, my dad was an effusive fan when hotels got it right. And would tell excited tales of superb service when he had it. For, instance at the Danieli in Venice. And I saw his eyes literally fill with tears when remembering the Swanage hotel manager who saved my parents from a nightmarish honeymoon with some well-placed kindness. It is stories like these on which great brands are built. As they say, 'a brand is the story playing in the customer's mind'. That said, my father also recognised he was, at times, an appalling customer. And he loved telling this self-deprecating story to prove it.

Cliffhanger

The last device I want us to consider is the cliffhanger. No better example of this than the final scene of *The Italian Job* where a coach filled with happy bank robbers and a ton of bullion spins out of control and is left, quite literally, hanging over a cliff while Michael Caine's character, Charlie, tries to sort things out:

Hold still, hold still. Nobody move. We're balancing right on the edge. Very slowly, move this way. Very slowly. Don't make a sharp movement. Come as far up this end as you can get. Watch it, watch it. Watch it, Bill! The gold is pulling it over the edge. We'll have to get it back. Get back! Get back! Now hold still. Don't move. Don't move at all. Don't no-one get out the door, neither. Otherwise we'll all go. Edge back as far as you can go, to cou... to counterbalance me. Now...

We want to see how he is going to resolve this impossible situation. Our minds teeter with the coach. But we know he will manage it because he's the star and this is a blockbuster film and those films end well, right? Wrong. The very last line of the film is Charlie saying:

Hang on a minute, lads. I've got a great idea.

And there we leave it. The camera pans away over the Alps and we are left – waiting for the sequel. It's dissatisfying but addictive. We want to know what happened – our brains require we complete that unfinished synaptic pathway, but the storyteller has delightfully frustrated us.

That's the tormenting power of the cliffhanger. It leaves your audience hooked. It's a technique that was often used by master tale-teller Charles Dickens whose novels were often published chapter by chapter in magazines. Dickens knew, as do the producers of series like *Homeland*, *Breaking Bad* and *Game of Thrones* today, that you always want to leave your audience wanting to know what happens next...

So, the final thing I want to tell you in this chapter, and it could be the most important point of all – the one that's really going to save your bacon when you are standing there in front of a room full of hostile shareholders or disgruntled staff is this...

TELLING TALES

Tales live or die in the telling. Here we look at techniques to help you tell engaging stories, whether you are a 'natural storyteller' or not. The key isn't presentation, it's narration.

Chapter 5

TELLING TALES

It doesn't surprise me that there is a whole industry devoted to helping professional people improve their presentation skills. This is a YouTube enabled age where everyone is in 'close-up' and there's a pressure to look like a confident performer. Fine if you're an extrovert who is comfortable in the limelight but it can be a real challenge if you aren't one of Nature's blabbermouths. Introverts are leaders too.

It's the word *presentation* I have a problem with.

It has attractive enough roots: *praesentare* meaning to 'place something before someone' and it spawned the idea of a 'present', literally placing a gift in the presence of someone.

If only the modern presentation was a gift! More

often it feels like a punishment – both to those who are asked to present and those in the audience. Presentation has come to mean a person standing in the dark clicking through PowerPoint slides as their colleagues – anything but present – squint at emails and watch the clock.

I would argue that a leader needs to cultivate the art not of presentation, but of *narration*; the ability to use story to cross the space between you and your audience and create meaning in their minds.

We've spent some time looking at how to construct those stories. Now let's look at how you stand there and tell your tale. I'll focus on five elements that are do-able and make you a more confident storyteller, whether you are a shy bunny or a show-off.

1. Start well

Storytellers think a lot about how to start. They know they have to hook the audience from the get-go. Take the opening of George Orwell's *1984*:

> It was a bright cold day in April and the clocks were striking thirteen.

We know from the first sentence that something is seriously awry with this world. Or the opening of *American Beauty*, where, over a long helicopter shot of a routine suburb, the narrator tells us:

My name is Lester Burnham. This is my neighbor-hood. This is my street. This is my life. I am 42 years old. In less than a year, I'll be dead.

The opening shot of a film has to be more important than the popcorn. The first bar of a symphony, the overture of an opera, the prologue to a play – they are all designed to nudge the everyday thinking of daily life and let us know something special, different, note-worthy is about to happen. Storytellers, particularly in the performing arts, know they are in competition for your attention and hone their openings accordingly.

In the business world, by contrast, it's perfectly normal for things not to begin at all but to stumble into life. Take the technical car crash that heralds the opening of a standard conference call:

'Hello, uh'
Beep
'David has joined the conference…'
'Hi, David, you've got Gill and Sue on the line and…'
'Can you speak up?'
Beep
'David has left the conference'
'Hello, Jo, can you speak up?'
'Hello…?
'Ok, I think she's in a cab. I guess we'd better…

Beep
'David has joined the conference'
'… begin.'

Leaders, listen up. If you are going to tell a story, particularly an important one – START WELL.

You aren't going to get a better moment to make a powerful impression and hook the audience than at the start.

Everyone talks about the iconic 'I have a dream' speech, but look how Martin Luther King started his famous address:

> *I am happy to join with you today in what will go down in history as the greatest demonstration for freedom in the history of our nation.*

Now that is what you call an opening!

When Steve Jobs launched the iPod in 2001 he used exactly the same attention demanding trumpet call:

> *We lured you here today with the promise of introducing a breakthrough digital device that's not a Mac… And that's exactly what we are going to do.*

Both in their way, were about to change the world – and, as story makers, they knew to pay attention to their openings.

'An opening line should say: Listen. Come in here. You want to know about this', says Stephen King, one of the world's most successful, popular and prolific authors.

The first sentence of *1984* ticks all the boxes. Other personal favourites of mine are:

> *You better not never tell nobody but God.* (*The Colour Purple* by Alice Walker)

You're instantly enrolled in the narrator's secret.

> *Since it's Sunday and it's stopped raining, I think I'll take a bouquet of roses to my grave.* (*Someone Has Been Disarranging These Roses* by Gabriel García Marquez)

Huh? You want to understand this puzzle.

> *Happy families are all alike, every unhappy family is unhappy in its own way.* (*Anna Karenina* by Leo Tolstoy)

We're instantly ushered behind the scenes of a tragic domestic set up.

> *There was no possibility of taking a walk that day.* (*Jayne Eyre by Charlotte Brontë*)

The dismal life of a frustrated heroine summed up in just ten hopeless words.

> *In my younger and more vulnerable years, my father gave me some advice I have been turning over in my mind ever since.* (*The Great Gatsby* by F. Scott Fitzgerald)

What is that advice? And why is he no longer vulnerable?

> *As Gregor Samsa awoke one morning from uneasy dreams he found himself transformed in his bed into a monstrous vermin.* (*Metamorphosis* by Franz Kafka)

A living nightmare begins.

> *All children, except one, grow up.* (*Peter Pan* by J.M. Barrie)

This is a children's story written for adults who don't want to grow up.

You're not reading this book so you become a great author. But if you want to be a great leader – START WELL.

Oh, and before we leave this topic, do remember a great way to start can be with silence. It's a time-honoured theatrical technique. Don't start until you have the audience's attention. If they're not *sitting comfortably* then don't *begin*. I adapted this technique for a friend of mine, Mark, who spends a lot of time talking to techie audiences and needs to grab their attention. Before he talks about his revolutionary but extremely user-friendly software he pauses for eight seconds. Then he begins with the words: 'That eight seconds is all it will take to upload our system'. Point made, without a word. In the words of the philosopher and pop singer Ronan Keating, 'You say it best when you say nothing at all'.

2. Be specific

The veteran script-writing teacher Robert Kee once told a class I was attending: 'A writer knows the names of things'. That was his way of telling us to be specific, not vague, with our language. The pen you are using isn't just a *pen*, it's a *1952 Waterman* or an *original Bic with the end chewed off*. It wasn't given to you as a child, it was *given to you by your Aunt Rachel on your fourteenth birthday*. You didn't just *put it down*, you *placed it on the fake walnut top of the kitchen table you just bought from the IKEA in Wembley*.

In story world, the things are specific not hazy.

If you're recounting an anecdote, it didn't happen 'sometime in the past'; it happened *last October* or *last Tuesday evening* or when you were *living in the outskirts of Leith in the late '80s between leaving college and getting your first job.* You weren't told something interesting by someone. Oh no. *Your accountant, Chris, told you the secret of their success.* What day were you born on? *It was Thursday or maybe a Friday.* What was the name of that hotel you visited on the trip to Malta? *The Imperial.*

And what if you can't remember all this?

You make it up.

That's the deal with fiction. We don't mind if you are wrong, we just don't want you to be hazy.

I learned this the hard way, in the rough and tumble of live improv. The worst crime you can perpetrate on an audience is haziness. Two unnamed people standing in an unspecified location talking generalities is the worst improv you can endure. I know, because, as a newbie, that's what I did.

'Hello'
'Hello'
'Nice here, isn't it'
'Mmm'
'Did you hear that?'
'What?'
'That. Oh it's stopped'

And so on. And on. And on.

On the other hand, watch two practised improvisers, and you'll instantly know the characters are, say, trainee accountants waiting outside a job interview and the sound was a cry of pain from the current interviewee within. Or Knights of Old sitting on a castle wall having lunch when suddenly they hear a dragon's roar. Or a father Mr Lovejoy and his son Barry, waiting outside the Maternity ward for the first cry of their new family member. Except it's not a baby's cry they hear – it's a dog's bark.

You get the idea. Give them detail. It can be fictional, sure. But not fuzzy.

Letting the audience know the basics of who, what, when and where makes for vivid storytelling. The more specific, the more believable.

Numbers game

That's why sales people use numbers. Numbers sound real. They lend validity to the sales story you are hearing. 75% of customers note a huge improvement? *I want one.* The bike is known to take five minutes off a 40k ride? *I want one of those too.* The 30cm radial is tuned to withstand an impact of 7.5 newton metres? *I don't even know what that means but I'm in.*

Specific numbers bring a bounce to your storytelling. You weren't set upon by some blokes, but by eight blokes. She hasn't had some husbands – *she has been through five.*

They also lend a real authority. Probably they shouldn't. You know what they say – sorry – you know what

Norman, a distinguished banker friend of mine once told me:

Numbers are either looked up or made up. And those that are looked up – are made up.

Despite the fact that numbers aren't facts, that statistics can easily be manipulated, that data is highly subjective, there's something compellingly real about using digits in your storytelling.

While I was writing this chapter we had an election in the UK which everyone knew was going to be 'too close to call'. We knew this because the pollsters told us. And pollsters deal with figures. When they say it's going to be 50/50 or, even more compellingly, 49.8/50.2, we believe the tale. And tale it turned out to be, when the Tories actually won by a sizeable majority.

More people live on the banks of the Yangtze than live in the USA. I don't know if it's true – or really care. It makes a good story.

I am not saying you should be wilfully inaccurate in your storytelling. I am saying that specificity makes for vivid storytelling, accurate or not. And 61% of Lithuanians would agree.

3. Be 3 – if not more – Dimensional

You're walking across the funky new atrium heading for an espresso and you see three members of your team hurrying to intercept you. None look happy. Clearly, it's time for a bit of leadership. One tells you:

I am feeling under pressure

Another says:

I can't see the light at the end of the tunnel

The third is also agitated:

From what I heard, it sounds to me like we're in trouble

What does this tell you – apart from the fact you should have walked faster? It tells you, you are dealing with three people who experience the world differently. The differences are subtle, but crucially important if you are going to create a story that is going to calm them down and allow you to get to your espresso.

I want to suggest we humans have three main ways of encoding data from the world around us. We see things. We hear things. And/or we feel things. Students of Neuro Linguistic Programming (NLP) would call these Visual, Auditory and Kinaesthetic. NLP says we all have our preferred representational system. And this is indicated by the words we use to describe the world. The person *looking for the light at the end of the tunnel* is probably a visual. The one hearing troubling things likely has an auditory bias. And the poor person *feeling* all that *pressure*, a kinaesthetic.

Clearly, we all use all three systems all the time, but listen to your colleagues' language – and your own – and you'll start hearing a default emerge.

So what? So when you are telling your stories make sure you include all three systems. Focus purely on visual language, go on and on about your vision and how things will look in the bright and colourful future you are picturing … and you just lost two thirds of your audience! Sight, sound and sensation are the primary colours of story. A skilled story maker uses all three to enthral the audience.

Aristotle, the grandmaster of rhetoric (he'd probably be called an *audience engagement specialist* if he was alive today) counselled something similar when he split the art of persuasion into three categories: logos (logic), ethos (character) and pathos (sympathy). Using these three levers you can win over your audience because when you speak, their response is:

You sound *logical. You* look *credible. It* feels *plausible.*

Open any great work of fiction and you'll see the three-way dance in action. Here, as an example, is the unforgettable storytelling moment where Charles

Dickens's young orphan, Oliver Twist, is bullied by the older boys at the workhouse to ask for more gruel!

The evening arrived; the boys took their places. The master, in his cook's uniform, stationed himself at the copper; his pauper assistants ranged themselves behind him; the gruel was served out; and a long grace was said over the short commons. The gruel disappeared; the boys whispered each other, and winked at Oliver; while his next neighbours nudged him. Child as he was, he was desperate with hunger, and reckless with misery. He rose from the table; and advancing to the master, basin and spoon in hand, said: somewhat alarmed at his own temerity:

'Please, sir, I want some more.'

The master was a fat, healthy man; but he turned very pale. He gazed in stupified astonishment on the small rebel for some seconds, and then clung for support to the copper. The assistants were paralysed with wonder; the boys with fear.

'What!' said the master at length, in a faint voice.

'Please, sir,' replied Oliver, 'I want some more.'

The master aimed a blow at Oliver's head with the ladle; pinioned him in his arm; and shrieked aloud for the beadle.

It's a piece of storytelling you can definitely hear, see and feel. And, if you read again, you'll see that's deliberate. Dickens shifts us expertly through the sensory gears like a Formula 1 driver...

[Visual]
The evening arrived; the boys took their places. The master, in his cook's uniform, stationed himself at the copper; his pauper assistants ranged themselves behind him; the gruel was served out;

[Auditory]
and a long grace was said over the short commons. The gruel disappeared; the boys whispered each other, and winked at Oliver;

[Kinaesthetic]
while his next neighbours nudged him. Child as he was, he was desperate with hunger, and reckless with misery. He rose from the table; and advancing to the master, basin and spoon in hand, said: somewhat alarmed at his own temerity:
'Please, sir, I want some more.'

[Visual]
The master was a fat, healthy man; but he turned very pale. He gazed in stupified astonishment on the small rebel for some seconds,

[Kinaesthetic]
and then clung for support to the copper. The as-
sistants were paralysed with wonder; the boys with
fear.

[Auditory]
'What!' said the master at length, in a faint voice.
'Please, sir,' replied Oliver, 'I want some more.'

[Kinaesthetic]
The master aimed a blow at Oliver's head with the
ladle; pinioned him in his arm; and

[Auditory]
shrieked aloud for the beadle.

The novelist and storytelling teacher Danny Scheinmann urges the business people he works with to think of facts like a hill covered with sheet ice. It's smooth and pristine but very tricky for the audience to climb. This sensory language provides footholds for them. Because it's emotional rather than rational.

Emotion is the attractive force that binds your audience to your story.

Human minds are irresistible copy-cats. We read an uplifting story, we feel elated. Someone describes or depicts something sad, we feel sad.

There are sound scientific reasons for this. The neuro-economist Paul Zak has shown that the brain will secrete the same empathy-inducing neuropeptide, Oxytocin, whether you physically meet an ailing child – or simply hear a story about one.[1]

The neuroscientist Tara Swart points out that it's not just empathy that can leap the space between minds in this way – pleasure too. And it's not just humans that can have vicarious experience.

She cites an experiment where monkeys were set tasks and rewarded with peanuts. The monkeys' neural activities were tracked as they shelled and ate the peanuts – and significant amounts of the neuro-transmitter dopamine were detected in the reward pathways of the brain. Dopamine is a key agent in the sensation of pleasure. During a break in the experiment, a technician shelled and ate some peanuts. As the monkeys watched this their own dopamine production kicked in, showing a monkey can vicariously experience pleasure seeing a human doing something it knows it would enjoy.

The brain literally lights up when you use the emotion-triggering vocabulary of seeing, hearing and feeling. And leaders that remember this have the ability to do something quite remarkable.

I think of it as Model Making.

Allow me to demonstrate by taking you to the door of my bedroom:

---

[1] In his book *The Moral Molecule*.

Yes, when I was a teenager growing up I had my own bedroom. I can see it now. It is the smallest bedroom in the house. The door swings open left to right. It's only about four paces to the sash-window in front of me, but it's made to feel more spacious, at least I think so, by the day-glo wallpaper I convinced my parents to hang. And by having my dad build my bed on top of a cupboard. There's a shelf with books and a cup with pens on the table. The sash-window is hard to open but if you yank it up you can hear ...

What? What can you hear? When you imagine my room – as you have been doing – what do you hear in the street? What's the weather like? What colour is that bright wallpaper? Does the bed have sheets or a duvet? How many pens sit in the cup and which books are on the shelf?

This is not a guessing game. I am not interested in whether you are accurate about how my bedroom looked and felt. Who cares? What I want you to do is look at *your* version of my room and notice that it is complete. You can mentally wander around it, look at posters on the wall, admire the wallpaper (lime green if you must know) read imagined book titles and then close the door behind you.

What just happened? Your brain did what it always does when it encounters a vivid description. It builds a model – its own model. It's not only a three dimensional spatial model, it's sensory too. It comes with temperatures, sounds, smells. A complete, believable reality.

I don't know about you, but I find that amazing. As far as we know sea anemones and spiny anteaters cannot do this. It's a unique trick of human neurology, one that storytellers exploit to the full.

It's how a book can get the hairs standing up on the back of your neck, make you laugh out loud on the tube, or reduce you to tears of sadness.

Back to Charles Dickens for a perfect example:

She was dead. No sleep so beautiful and calm, so free from trace of pain, so fair to look upon. She seemed a creature fresh from the hand of God, and waiting for the breath of life; not one who has lived and suffered death … Dear, gentle, patient, noble Nell was dead.

The words seem sentimental to us today but back in February 1841, when Dickens released this climactic chapter of his serialised novel, *The Old Curiosity Shop*, there was nearly a public riot. Readers had been petitioning to him for weeks, pleading that Little Nell, the book's ailing orphan heroine, be allowed to live. Even Dickens struggled with the decision to kill off his beloved character: 'I am breaking my heart over this story'. One of the nation's leading judges, Lord Jeffrey, was found weeping over his copy, admitting: 'I am a great goose to have given way so, but I could not help it'. And when English ships docked in American ports people shouted out: 'Is Little Nell dead?'

Riots. Blubbing Lords. International outcry. All over the death of a character who everyone knew was never actually ALIVE! But story trumps biology. Our conscious minds know she's fiction – but to our unconscious minds Nell is as real as a member of our own family. The readers had built their living model of Dickens's fictional creation in their own minds. To kill that character was to destroy the model, leaving a painful void. And the readers genuinely grieved her loss. I felt the same when *Breaking Bad* came to an end. So strong is the power of a plausible and emotionally engaging fiction.

Never mind surround-sound and 3D video helmet, stories are the ultimate virtual reality technology. As I often tell my son – while I am prying his fingers from the PlayStation controller and trying to get him to read instead – story books are the video games of the mind.

And that, as a leader, is something you want to remember. If you want to engage the audience, describe a world in which they can build their own version. A deeply imagined, see-able, feel-able, hear-able model of the world. And you will have connected it in ways that no spreadsheet on earth will ever allow.

Information is something that has to be actively remembered. That's why a succession of dry facts is quickly forgotten. But when you help the audience build a three dimensional model in their mind, your model becomes theirs. And is likely to remain woven into their thinking.

As the saying goes: 'If you build it *they* will come. If they build it, they will stay!'

4. Time

The early bird gets the worm but the second mouse gets the cheese. (Willie Nelson)

It dominates our working lives, most particularly the scarcity of it.

Wouldn't it be great, as a leader, to be able to command time. To override the laws of physics, to have time move at the speed you want. To be able to shoot into the future and then back into the past at the blink of an eye. To slow time down almost to a standstill so you can appreciate the minute details of the moment. Or accelerate at lightning speed across the weeks, months and years so we can grasp the broad sweep of what's really happening.

Fiction allows you to do that. When you start making stories, not presenting plans, time can become your friend, one of your greatest assets.

Right tale, right time

'Most of what makes a book "good" is that we are reading it at the right moment for us', says Alain de Botton.

Ever had the feeling that the radio is talking to you? Not in the schizophrenic 'voices in my head' sense. More that the sappy love song being sung is exactly appropriate for the new person in your life. Or the heart rending break-up song, while corny, seems apt when a relationship ends. My teenage daughter feels Taylor Swift's songs perfectly and spookily articulate what's going on in her own life. My teenage son probably feels the same about AC/DC.

Some songs gain huge significance and power for us when we hear them at the right time. Stories are the same.

One well-timed, relevant anecdote can stay with you your whole life.

The opposite is also true. Poor timing can make your storytelling not just unhelpful but counterproductive.

Poor timing includes:

- When people don't have time, attention or willingness to listen.
- When the audience is wanting to get gritty and operational.
- When you have already told one (or more) stories before and risk becoming a story bore. CEOs beware of this one.
- When the story is at the wrong time of day. You wouldn't tell a child an adrenalin-pumping horror story to get them to sleep at the end of the day. Don't

tell a team a sleep inducing one at the beginning of the day (or week, or year).

- Telling a long story when a short one will do.

The key is to have your attention on your audience. How much appetite do they have for the story you are telling? When they switch off, so should you. The best time to stop is, ideally, just before they run out of attention. The good news is, the better you tell it, the more time you have.

If in doubt, ask them. I love to do this when I am doing a speech or session. I'll take people to a cliffhanging moment in a story and ask: 'Do you want me to go on?' You usually get a big 'yes' from a group of people sitting forward in their seat in the dark, just like our ancestors around those winter fires ...

Right story, right time. This is the mantra of story-tellers through the ages. Which is why they have developed a huge variety of different story types – and lengths – for different occasions. Which brings us to ...

Right time scale

So, *right story, right time*. And let's add *right length*. If you want to engage your audience you have to tailor your story length to the situation. If you're the bard of a Stone Age tribe, you'll want a story that unfolds night after night around the campfire. You want to eke out the tale like the ancient equivalent of the HBO box set. It's this hugely expansive storytelling that generates epic fables like the *Iliad* and the *Odyssey*, *Beowulf* and the 200,000 line-long narrative poem the *Mahabharata*.

Timing is situational.

If you are telling a tale round a fire, each episode needs to fit into the period between lighting the campfire and the tribe peeling off to go to sleep.

A stand-up comedian, on the other hand, who needs to be able get a laugh a minute is going to adjust the tempo and length of their tale-telling accordingly.

Two cannibals eating a clown.
One asks the other: 'This taste funny to you?'

Short, by the way, doesn't mean less rich than long. Many authors will tell you a short story is actually far harder to write than a long one. The shortest story I know of is the one Ernest Hemingway produced in response to his own challenge. He bet his literary lunch companions at the The Algonquin Hotel $10 that he could write a novel in just six words. They took the bet and he scribbled the following on a napkin:

For Sale: baby shoes, never worn.

It's a piece of virtuoso storytelling that pares away all unnecessary wordage and socks you in the heart with a tragic single line.

In the busy world of business, attention is in short supply. So have some short stories in your back pocket to use in a brief chat or call.

Be chron-illogical

When you present a plan it's sensible to do it in chrono-logical order, right? You start at today and work through to a fixed point in the future. Step one. Step two. Step three. Sensible. But BORING.

Fiction, happily allows you to be much more creative with time. You're freed from chrono-logic. Past, present and future are your playthings. Yes the story usually ends at a later point in time than it started, but you can play all sorts of games with time on the way.

Think about all those films that start at the final scene and then loop back in time (via the wonderful cinematic device of flashback) to explain how you got there. *Sunset Boulevard* is a classic example. It opens with a corpse floating in a glamorous swimming pool and the narrator (the voice of the victim) invites us to learn what happened to put him there. *Citizen Kane*, likewise, starts with the death of the hero and then flashes back to his childhood. You've hooked the audience from the start. They know where they will end up, but only learn over time how they get there.

How does a leader use this time travelling quality of narrative to get a message across with real power?

Travel back in time with me for a moment. It's a wet

and windy November morning in 1863. A field in Philadelphia. You're looking out over an audience that's cold, wet and bored. They have just stood through a two hour speech by a famously verbose orator (Edward Everett). You've got about two minutes to make your point. And you have to make it count.

You're the President of a country that's in civil war – a war that's turning out to be a lot more costly and bloody than anyone anticipated. This is why you've come here – to the site of a battlefield where 50,000 soldiers died – to convince the audience, and the nation, the war is worth it. Your entire credibility – and that of the United States experiment – hangs on the next two minutes.

What do you do? Hint: don't give them a presentation.

Tell them a story.

Fourscore and seven years ago …

That's how Abraham Lincoln started the most famous two-minute piece of storytelling in history.

It's the classic use of time-slip. Instead of starting on this overcast and rainy day, he shoots us back 90 years to a point in the past:

… our fathers brought forth on this continent a new nation, conceived in liberty, and dedicated to the proposition that all men are created equal.

In leadership terms, he is creating context. He is saying to his audience *this is important and here's why*. Having established this crucial piece of backstory, Lincoln brings us to the present:

> *Now we are engaged in a great civil war, testing whether that nation, or any nation so conceived and so dedicated, can long endure ...*

Having established that the stakes are higher, he now zips forward in time to a distant future when ...

> *... this nation, under God, shall have a new birth of freedom – and that government of the people, by the people, for the people, shall not perish from the earth ...*

In just two minutes – and just 272 words – Lincoln has told a tale spanning centuries. A dispiritingly grey day seems a pivotal moment when a daring experiment in the past gets tested. If the audience can rise to the challenge they will secure a bright and noble future. Inspiring stuff. And, with it, Lincoln changed the course of history. Not with a plan. But with a story.

'But how does that apply in a business context?' I imagine you asking. 'I don't need to take a nation to war, David, I just want to excite my audience about a new product, program or project'.

Here's a way of using narrative time travel that I heard at a recent Tech Accelerator event. The speaker had 90 seconds to pitch his product, a radically new, web-based approach to the bond market.

He could have plunged straight into some logical presentation format like the hackneyed old:

- *Tell them what you are going to tell them*
- *Tell them*
- *Tell them what you told them*

Fortunately, he didn't. Instead he opened his story in the near future, painting the picture of a huge part of the finance industry – the Bond Market – that was about to be disrupted. Then, instead of introducing his product, he telescoped back in time – very cinematic of him – to seven months ago, when he was not an entrepreneur but a successful bond trader in one of the planet's most prosperous financial houses. 'But then', he told us, 'I had this idea …' He fast-forwards to the present, showing the idea taking shape, picking up momentum and investors. He then jumped forward three years into the future to give a mouthwatering picture of the new firm's likely growth, market share and returns. He didn't finish there, but returned, cleverly, to the present moment by announcing the signing, that very morning, of the firm's first million pound customer. Cue standing ovation.

Chron-illogical. But very effective.

Even closer to home, imagine you want to inspire your team about what the coming year holds.

You could, for example, walk them month by month through what they can expect. They'll be on their email – if not actually asleep – by the time you reach September. Or …

You could start in the present, zoom forward to the end of their careers where you picture them looking back at this year as one of the best they have ever had. Then you could rewind 12 months and give a hint of the great place you'll all be four quarters from now. And what it will mean. That reminds you of something two decades ago when the company was forming and the mission it had then. At that time you were still at school, dreaming of making a difference in the world. And that's what you're aiming to have achieved 365 days from now. Again, you picture the team standing on the same spot, a year older and a year more experienced, more fulfilled. And once people can really feel that, you can work backwards to the present day, describing the excitements and difficulties that lie between now and then.

OK, it's disorientating but that's intentional. As a leader you'll sometimes need to first disorientate people, shake them loose from those everyday stories (of Fear, Fantasy and Formula) if you are to re-orientate them in a more helpful, creative, productive, imaginative direction.

It's time to move on. It would be sadly ironic if a

section on time management went on too long! But before we do, one quick extra point:

Jump in!

There's a scriptwriting mantra in Hollywood that goes: 'enter late, leave early'. It's reminding the writer not to include any more information than is necessary in a scene. Get into the scene as late as you can. You don't need to show the murderer putting on their socks, getting into their car, driving across town, parking, feeding the meter, walking up to the young victim's door and knocking. Start with the knock on the door. The same applies to the end of the scene. As soon as essential action has happened, get out. Movies are expensive to make so film-makers tend to pare things down to their essentials. It also makes the storytelling more dynamic.

As a leader, take a look at the 20 slide pack you have prepared – and cut the first seven slides. Think about what the audience really needs to hear and jump in there.

The hugely popular and incredibly readable American crime writer Elmore Leonard has published his *10 Rules of Good Writing*. Number 10 is: 'Try to leave out what readers tend to skip.'

Quite.

5. It's personal

'A leader is best when people barely know he exists', said the ancient Chinese philosopher Lao Tzu. 'When his work is done, his aim fulfilled, they will say: we did it ourselves'. He was making the point that successful leadership is about people doing want you want them to but feeling they have done it voluntarily and independently.

As a senior and very effective civil servant once confided to me: 'You can get anything done in this world – provided you don't want to take credit.'

I say this because a lot of people I meet confuse leadership with charisma. They point to the natural storytellers with the (apparently) easy public manner and feel they can't be an effective leader unless they copy that style.

Not so. Some of the most powerful leaders I know are significantly modest. Even shy. So if you don't think of yourself as a high wattage extrovert, take heart.

That said, you aren't going to get very far unless you are very personally invested in your leadership. When you are with people they want to know who you are and that you are authentic.

I think of this as *Less Me, More I*. Effective leadership isn't about ego (me, me, me) but it absolutely is about who you are as a person, what you stand for and – if necessary – what you'd fight for. That's what I mean by the 'I'.

This is where story helps you enormously. When you recount a story, you're naturally more engaged than you are when reciting figures. And this automatically makes you more engaging.

Try this in front of a mirror. Or a pet. Talk for 60

seconds about share prices or something very analytical. Then take 60 seconds to tell the story of your favourite holiday. Even a goldfish will find the second more naturally interesting. When you recount a real experience we are not just learning the facts, we are also learning about you.

You may not be interested in people learning about you. You may be one of those low-key types that dials down their personality and thinks your ideas should speak for themselves. But here's a heads-up for leaders everywhere …

Whenever you tell a story, your audience hears *two*. There's the story that's being told. *And* there's the story of the person telling the story.

Remember your teachers at school? They stood in front of us for hours telling their tales. And while they did, we made up tales – usually lurid and sensational – about them. While the subjects they taught us are probably quite rusty now, I bet you remember the gossip like it was yesterday.

People are not just curious about your story, but about you. You can try to avoid this – and I have seen many leaders try – behind a smooth wall of professionalism. Dress formal, read from a lectern, stick to the facts. It doesn't really work. Your people are still making up stories about you; *he's aloof … a cold fish … something to hide … clearly she's not interested in people, just numbers… what's she scared of?*

Far better to show who you are through the stories you tell.

Which reminds me – the power of anecdotes

If you want to bring a point to life, do it with an anecdote. 'This reminds me of a time when …' It is effective if these micro stories are about people rather than things. 'I was in Jakarta last month and I met a manager there called Anggun …' It is helpful if they are also true. Which is why I encourage the leaders I work with to collect real stories every day. When you are out and about, talk to people. Listen to their tales. Remember their names. They don't have to be epic stories. Human scale anecdotes about real people are very effective.

And you don't need to restrict your anecdotes to the business sphere. When you tell an anecdote about your family or friends (make sure it's not libellous) you are telling people about who you really are, puncturing the professional mask, and people really appreciate that from their leaders.

As an aside, Charles Handy has a gentle but wonderfully searching question he delights in asking the business leaders he meets: 'So who are you pretending to be?' We are all pretending. And the professional persona is just as much a fiction as any other. What people really appreciate from you as a leader is a glimpse of your authentic self.

The good news is, when you dip into your personal

archive for story material you can do away with the teleprompter and the PowerPoint (which is basically a memory aid in disguise). Experiences that have happened to you and which you have embodied are much easier to remember than information you are trying to remember.

You don't need to work hard to remember the feeling of waves lapping at your feet on the beach. You do, if I ask you to remember what was written on page 15. Personal, embodied memories seem burned into our hard disks where pure information seems to be stored in RAM (rapid access memory), which, like a computer's, can be temperamental, hard to navigate and occasionally just crashes for no reason.

The other bonus of harvesting stories from your own life is that you can bin those Body Language for Presentations manuals. When you recall a personal experience in rich detail a part of your mind travels back there and recreates what you saw, heard and felt. It's why you laugh again when you replay an amusing moment, or tear up when you bring a sad episode to mind.

This is gold dust when it comes to engaging your audience. As you re-experience the highs and lows, they will too. Though they may not realise it, their neurology will be mirroring, however subtly, your emotions. Tara Swart explains:

When someone is talking to us, telling us a story, we detect micro muscular changes in their face. We

*run these through a part of our brain which con-
tains what we call mirror neurons. Here, without
realizing, we mimic the movements to some extent
and this tells us how we would feel if we were making those expressions. This mirroring is the basis of
empathy.*

Stories are, then, key to creating empathy with your public, audience or team.

But don't overdo it. Different cultures have different
appetites for personal disclosure. And don't do this cyn-
ically – like politicians at election time choking back the
tears to win your vote. People are wise to that. If you
want to come across as an authentic leader, the rule of
thumb is be authentic.

Anchoring is key

Do you know the song 'Silence is Golden'? If you don't,
you haven't missed much. It's a corny pop song sung in
the '60s by The Tremeloes (in paisley shirts, tie-dye and
alarming helmet haircuts). I don't want to like it, but
there's a synapse in my mind that is devoted to that song
and every time I hear it, it projects me back to being
seven years old again. I'm the same with the smell of
Mitsouko (a fling in the '90s), the taste of freshly baked
baguette (Paris family holiday in the '70s) and the
opening bars of the third act of Tosca (makes my heart
beat double because my mind instantly shoots me back

to when I was an 11-year-old boy soprano about to sing at the Royal Opera House ...).

That's the thing about anchors. We all have them. Sensory triggers that are inextricably associated with past experiences. They anchor us to our memories and we're hopeless to resist when someone fires them off for us.

Anchoring – the process of associating an internal response with some external or internal trigger so that the response may be quickly, and sometimes covertly, re-accessed – is a practice that can be used powerfully by stage hypnotists, great teachers, proponents of Neuro-Linguistic Programming (NLP) and, if you are smart, the storytelling leader.[2]

Why? Because anchoring helps make sure the story you just told is actually going to be remembered. Very helpful I think you will agree, particularly in business where there's so much to remember, very little is.

Anchoring is a complex skill. I can't do it justice here but I will share two simple ways to help anchor your narrative in the audience's mind.

The first is possibly too obvious. Make sure they enjoy themselves. If the audience is having a good time – if they associate your story with pleasure – they are much more likely to remember what you said.

The second is to anchor your tale with a prop or object. Let me give you a real life example that concerns a

---

[2] Description by Robert Dilts, one of the originators of NLP.

young leader, Sangeeth, and a very important conference.

It was convincing but not compelling. Like a lot of presentations in today's business world, Sangeeth's was heavy on ideas but slight on impact. It was evident he was passionate about his subject – sustainable, low-cost housing – but in today's crowded attention market, *evidence* is not enough to make a case. Sangeeth was about to talk at an international conference for the world's leading infrastructure 'doers'. He didn't want them to *agree*, he wanted them to *act*. And his slot was just ten minutes long.

The stakes were high. And Sangeeth asked me to fly out to the Emirates and work with him so he could make a lasting impression.

I asked him to tell me more. Not more *what* – there were ample facts and figures – more *why*. Why was affordable, low-cost housing so important to the world – and to him? What was his story?

He took me back to one of the formative experiences of his childhood in a small town in India, the moment his family moved for the first time into a house of their own. As he spoke with quiet intensity, the office disappeared and we were back in that low-cost home, watching his parents receiving the house key from the local Holy Man and then seeing his mother, in her new kitchen, symbolically boiling that key in milk and wiping away a tear of joy.

Technically, the key wasn't the priest's to give but

where Sangeeth comes from, the symbolic hand-over underscores the idea that this house (where his parents still live) was 'a gift from the Gods'.

That key represented security, stability and above all a sense of identity, which for Sangeeth is the single most potent by-product of having a home to call your own.

I advised Sangeeth to stop fretting about slides and ask his mother to send that key so he could use it in the presentation. I suggested he should tell his personal story and, at the appropriate moment, take his mum's key out of his pocket.

That's exactly what he did. Apparently you could hear a pin drop.

'This is what sustainable housing is about.' Sangeeth told the world's policy makers. 'Not houses, but this ... identity. Let's create a million of these.'

And he laid the key on the lectern with a faint click as the audience applauded.

It's hardly special effects, but the key gives the mind a physical object to anchor the conceptual message. It's what we call in NLP an 'analogue marker', a physical correlate to an idea that makes it more memorable. An anchor.

But there's more to this than fancy technique. I think our flat screen, digital world hungers for three-dimensional reality.

When the British Museum wanted to engage its millennial audience, it launched a hugely ambitious and very successful campaign called History of the World in 100 Objects. In it the Museum's director, Neil MacGregor, sought to retell humanity's story in 100 15-minute broadcasts, each one focusing on an artefact (be it grand or humble) from the museum's vast collection and telling their tale.

Millions of listeners heard the podcasts, spawning a bestselling book and a nationwide teaching program. As so often happens in this virtual reality, hall-of-mirrors age of ours, the series itself became a story. Which objects should or should not be included? The debate raged over mealtimes and around water-coolers. The makers deliberately left the final object open to fan the flames, asking the public to decide. Would it be an iPad? Or a Botox needle? For the record, the 'winning' final object was a solar powered light that could change the lives of families with no electricity.

Apparently, object based learning is more compelling than ever in this increasingly screen based world of ours. There's something compelling about *real* objects and the real stories they embody. They don't just tell the story. They bring the story to life.

Months later, people are still referring to Sangeeth as the 'key guy'. It's not just because of what he said, but (to paraphrase Maya Angelou) they *remember how he made them feel.*

Sangeeth's key brought the daily reality of homelessness into a plush international conference hall. He turned a concept into a reality. And changed – just a little – how people understand the world. Homes aren't just about housing they are about identity.

Sometimes a key *is* the key.

SO...

Practice #3: How's it going?

Don't wait for the formal presentation or the big speech to practise the techniques in this book. If you really pay attention, you'll start seeing opportunities to tell stories everywhere. In the corridor, the lift, the shop floor, the canteen, the street...[1]

How many times a day does someone ask 'how's it going?' And how often do you mumble something about 'OK' or 'fine'? Or worse, 'can't complain'. This last answer, beloved of the British, actually means 'I have lots to complain about and would but I won't because I don't think you're really interested and even if you were nothing could be done...' There's a whole story in that two-word phrase. An unhelpful, energy sapping one.

---

[1] One of the most skilled leaders I know always refuses the high status corner office in favour of the one nearest the toilets. This way he knows he'll have more opportunities to encounter other leaders and plant helpful narratives in their minds.

Here's a little something to help you turn a common-place social ritual into story gold.

You'll need a partner for this. Their job's easy. They just ask you the question 'how's it going?' repeatedly. And each time you try to tell a micro-story – a phrase or two – which paints a picture in their mind that they will remember.

For example:

'Great. Did you see what Clare and Yves have just achieved?'

'The team's really up against it but we've never done anything so ambitious before.'

'I've nearly cracked something which has been troubling me for ages…'

'To be honest I'm a bit overwhelmed at the moment – can I ask you for some advice…'

'I don't know what happened. I've never had such an enjoyable time.'

'Frankly it's a perfect storm. All hands on deck.'

'Given where we started in the summer? – AMAZING!'

You can refine this practice by changing the role your partner is playing. They're your boss, a new recruit, a member of the press, a customer, a disgruntled member of your team... Each time, think of a helpful 'story seed' you could plant. Consider:

- What would be helpful for them to know?
- What is my intention in telling them? ... to inspire, reassure, provoke, enrol, befriend, energise, stimulate, awaken, entertain, cheer up, alert, productively irritate ...

Try it!

FUTURE HACK

 There are already lots of stories in our minds about the future ... and few of them are ours. We have been 'future hacked'. By our parents, education, politicians, society, nation and culture. In many senses our future is already written – by other people. It's time to re-write what lies ahead.

Chapter 6

FUTURE HACK

The best way to predict the future is to create it. (Peter Drucker)

I don't know about you, but the future is important to me. I am going to be spending the rest of my life there. And my concern is that decisions about the future are being made right now by people I don't particularly trust.

It's not because they are bad people – OK, some are – but because the decisions they are taking are dictated by the stories in their minds. And they are not great stories. They are, as we have seen, stories of fear, fantasy and formula. Stories of ambition and greed. Primal, cave-dweller stories. Nationalistic stories of monsters under the bed and bogeymen leaping out of cupboards to threaten our way of life. Stories designed to lull us to sleep so others can make their self-serving choices while we slumber.

Which brings us to the real reason I wrote this book.

I'll tell you about it in a moment, but right now there's someone I want to introduce you to …

He's a young, bear-like man in jeans and a black t-shirt. And he is talking about his retirement plans. He intends to spend his final years on Mars. It sounds like an outrageous fantasy, but Elon Musk is perfectly serious. The billionaire entrepreneur behind PayPal and Tesla has set up a space travel company called SpaceX. He already has his own rocket, the Dragon, built at a fraction of the cost that NASA could manage. Oh, and gallon for gallon, it's cheaper to run than your car.

His declared goal is to 'make humanity interplanetary' as a way of increasing the odds that human consciousness survives in the universe. And when he talks about retiring off this planet, he is not only serious, but practical. 'I want to die on Mars', he says, adding with an engineer's precision, 'just not on impact.'

Musk has pictured not only the end of his life, but beyond – where his legacy will lead and what it may mean for others. Yes, he's a business person, but he is busy to an end that is greater than the bottom line: 'I think life on Earth must be about more than just solving problems … It's got to be something inspiring even if it is vicarious. When the US landed on the moon it was for all humanity. We count that as a human achievement.'

I mention him because we are just about to arrive at what, for me, is the heart of this book. I call it 'Authoring the Future'. It's an invitation to take everything you have learnt about making story and apply it as a tool to shape the future. That's right, story isn't just a way of *describing* what happens, but also of *creating* what happens.

Look how Musk is using story to help him realise his vision.

He's not a naturally gregarious guy. He's gone on record saying he'd rather stick a fork in his own hand than talk about his private life. 'I had to learn to be a little more extroverted,' he says. 'Ordinarily, I would sit in design meetings all day, exchanging ideas with people. But if I don't tell the story then it doesn't get out, and I want to try and get public support for extending life beyond Earth.'

Will Elon Musk make it to Mars? Or crash to earth like a 21st century Icarus – a rusting Iron Man? We don't yet know how this particular narrative will turn out. The point, for me, is that Musk's story is generating real change. People are thinking differently about what's possible. Space flight is no longer the preserve of the mega corporations. Real rockets, built by hipsters with a 'why not?' attitude are taking shape in the SpaceX hangers.

NASA is knocking on the door to learn how Musk fuels his craft for less than the cost of gasoline.[1]

And that's after Musk made safe payment on the internet (PayPal) commonplace and reinvented the electric car so it was practical and sexy (Tesla).

Musk is an instinctive Future Author. His narrative isn't just describing the world, it is changing the world. It's not a plan of the future. It's not a Gant chart. It's a story. One that other people can connect with, internalise and make their own. His story is making the future happen.

Authoring the future is powerful. It's also rare.

Few of us have (or give ourselves) time to think about what's coming so creatively and then actively create a narrative of our future. Have you?

What do you want to do with the rest of your life?
What do you want it to have been about?
When, where and how are you thinking of dying?

These are questions I like to spring on groups I meet around the world. Very few people give a detailed answer. It's usually a vague compilation of index-linked pensions, picture perfect tropical locations and a generalised loving haze – with the occasional champagne pop and distant gospel choir backing track.

---

[1] For the record, he does it by using a cheap derivative of Kerosene.

We keep it vague because these are unsettling, existential questions which we'd rather not consider.

And anyway, we are far too busy obsessing about what is just around the corner. That's what we're hard-wired to do. Our survival depends on it. For our primal ancestors, that snap of a twig in the undergrowth could mean we are going to have our next meal. Or that we are going to be the next meal.

Our ancestors visited oracles, consulted soothsayers, scanned the heavens and combed through the guts of dead chickens, all to get a heads up about what was coming next.

Faced with the unknowable, we humans tend to get panicky. We become what I call Future Tense.

Future Tension tends to curtail our creativity and limit our imagination. It diminishes our options and, from what I have seen of working life, actually makes us less intelligent.

Future Tension is behind the promising young project that gets squelched before it has a chance to prove itself. And also behind the dumb, wasteful project that you carried on doing way too long because it was in the plan.

Every organisation I have worked with suffers – to a greater or lesser extent – from Future Tension. As do their leaders.

Oh, they may put a brave face on it, but underneath they are whistling in the dark – suffering the pangs of Future Tension and hoping no-one notices.

Meet the hackers!

One of the more disturbing effects of being Future Tense is it makes us very susceptible to other people who claim to know what lies ahead for us because they have an interest in inserting *their* ideas into *our* future. I think of this as 'future hacking'. And everyone is doing it.

Politicians do it ...

Every politician in every election is to a greater or lesser degree asking you to trade your vote now for their promise of a better life in the future. It's always a 'vote for change'. Things can only get better. Together, we are assured, we CAN.

You'd think we'd wise up, but we're suckers for future certainty.

As an occasional expat in Italy, I enjoy sitting on the sideline, watching the opera of Italian politics unfold.

As I write, Silvio Berlusconi, the bunga bunga maestro himself, is out of the headlines. But I wouldn't write him off. For I have yet to see a more accomplished Future Hacker.

I remember watching the television when 'Il Principe' was down but not yet out. He was assuring his followers 'to have courage, things will get better ...' Italians are justifiably uncertain about their rickety economy and, despite the fact that Berlusconi was responsible for much of the chaos, they were lapping it up. 'I will not desert you' he assures the crowd, a flinty leader that will not budge (*io non mollo!*).

If you were thinking this is all very reminiscent of someone – Mussolini – you'd be right. Silvio even wore a black shirt on the podium to underline the point.

By the time this book is published Berlusconi may well be back in the driving seat. But even if he's serving a jail term, another political Future Hacker will be peddling their fables of stability-to-come in return for votes.

Advertisers do it …

Right now lovers around the world are proposing to each other. And shortly – provided she/he says yes – they will hit the jewellery stores looking for a diamond engagement ring.

Why?

There's nothing in law, literature or religious dogma that specifies spouses-to-be need an engagement ring of any kind, never mind a diamond one. Again, we've been future hacked, this time for commercial reasons.

In 1948, the South African mining giants, De Beers, found they had a surplus of diamonds on their hands. Diamonds are actually not that rare and De Beers were looking for a way to boost their market value.

So a bright spark had a cheeky idea. Why not make diamonds a must-have for fiancées? Their advertising campaign, which launched in 1948, 'Diamonds Are Forever', was one of the most successful in history. Speaking directly to the Future Tension of two people taking a blind chance on each other, the ads cheekily associated the durability of diamonds (the hardest substance on Earth) with the durability of marriage (one of the most delicate). Buy this, goes the inferred promise, and your love will last forever. I don't believe there's any evidence to prove this – but that doesn't stop us buying them. And making De Beers very rich into the bargain.

Another famous campaign which trades brilliantly on our Future Tension is Patek Philippe's. 'You never actually own a Patek Philippe. You merely look after it for the next generation' claim their ads, usually with a father and son portrait.

However schmaltzy the idea seems, it evidently works. Human beings are one of the few creatures on Earth that know they are going to die. And this scares them. Men particularly. Here's a company telling us their timepiece is actually timeless; you are not buying a product, you are investing in a legacy which will outlive you and benefit your loved ones for generations to come [cue soaring string orchestra and film of scudding clouds].

Immortality comes with a price tag – £5.5 million for the most expensive Patek Philippe yet sold – but clearly some people think that's a reasonable sum to cheat death, and it's a lot less costly or time-consuming than building yourself a pyramid.

And talking of monumental sums …

Businesses do it ...

In 2015 the global insurance industry was worth more than $5 trillion. The entire sector is based on Future Tension and our desire to control an unknown future. That was the case when Chinese traders first came up with the idea in 2000BC and it's the case today. We don't like the idea bad things will happen. But, as a senior insurance leader confided to me, what we like even less is the idea we will look stupid when misfortune does strike.

It's the fear of embarrassment that gets us signing on the dotted line for policies that – more than likely – we will never claim on.

Insurers are trading on our Future Tension, as do the banking, investment, pharmaceutical, fashion, real estate, tourism, defence, health, lottery and cosmetic surgery industries. It's a future hack of gold rush proportions!

The media does it ...

The much publicised 'millennium bug' did not cause a global meltdown on 1 January 2000. Avian Flu did not decimate us in 2005. GM food has not turned us all blue and the guitar band did not die after Oasis split up. Despite what the papers, TV and blogosphere might have predicted, none of these dire predictions came true. But that does not stop our media making them. Because they know we are Future Tense. And they can make millions feeding that tension further.

When, by the way, did news stop being about what

happened and start focussing on what the pundits say might happen? It's hard to imagine in the world of the 24 hour a day news cycle, but there was a time when news hungry meant someone in a pinch-backed leather armchair opening a copy of The Times (ironed) and reading for the first time the 'news' about an earthquake that had rocked China six months previously. It wasn't particularly new information. But at least it was historical. Today, information about any event (let's call it 'i') generates an i^3 amount of pontification, punditry and prediction about what will happen next.

It's surmise dressed as fact. The papers, TV channels and digital platforms are quite brazen about the fictional basis of their product. Hell, they even call the news items 'stories'.

Our parents do it ...

Bless them. They mean well. But parents just can't help planting their ideas into our future. I know I can't resist. And it's effective. How many of us are living a life that our parents wanted us to live? Or the complete opposite? Either way, did we really choose our occupations, residences and even partners without being profoundly influenced by their view of us?

A slew of Asian children are currently heading toward either engineering or medicine because they are the 'only' professions recognised by their parents. One high-flying consultant I know took weeks to pluck up courage and confess to his parents he had – disappointingly – been elected to one of the premier service firms on the planet. Apparently, the parents are still in mourning.

I know my father's own yearning for academia was in no small way responsible for me finding myself at Cambridge. Many of the people I meet in business are living a future that was predetermined by their parents' expectations. One client, Rajiv, a successful petrochemical consultant, put it succinctly when he said: 'I have spent 30 years living my parents' life. Now it's time for me.'

Our schools do it ...

Nothing fuels Future Tension like having children. Schools know this and position themselves as potential guarantors of your little one's future. It's a future hack of the education kind. And we buy it – sometimes to an obscene extent. I am thinking of New Yorkers grooming three-year-olds to get them into intensely contested places at pre-schools that promise a fast track from playpen to Ivy League. Worse still, the chic West London nursery where expectant mothers are known to elect for caesarean deliveries on dates that put them on pole position on the waiting list.

We sense this is a con. If you look around you'll see that many schools are actually preparing children for jobs that won't exist by the time they hit the job market. But because we are playing the educators' narrative, we fall for it, yet again paying for someone to replace our unease with their certainty.

Schools are also a favourite recruiting centre for those committed future hackers who have an interest in shaping our sense of national identity and enrolling us in conflict. That would include the zealots, ideologues and fundamentalists of all creeds, faiths, politics and colour. If a battle cannot be won in this generation, goes their thinking, ensure the children will continue fighting for it in the next.

For these committed future hackers, the beauty of school is that they can get to young minds when they are still malleable – what Robert Anton Wilson calls *imprint vulnerable*. Put a story in a textbook and – ta DAH! – it becomes fact.

You see this in conflict areas like the Middle East where both Israeli and Palestinian educators routinely use highly subjective storytelling in supposedly objective teaching materials.

The most comprehensive study (2009–12) found that 75% of Israeli textbooks and 81% of Palestinian ones described the 'other' as an 'enemy'.

One Israeli state school textbook referred to Arabs as 'masses of the wild nation'. Another called Israel 'a little lamb in a sea of seventy wolves'. Palestinian books include their own negative narrative about the 'Zionist occupation' and the 'usurpation of Palestine'. Some Palestinian books used the word 'Nakba' or *catastrophe* to describe the creation of the Jewish State in 1948 and were subsequently removed from Israel's Arab schools by the Israeli Education Ministry. This sparked a new wave of disagreement between those who saw it as the removal of damaging propaganda and those defending free speech.

One person's terrorist is another person's freedom fighter, right? It depends on the narrative perspective.

'When a leader says something, not everyone is listening' says Daniel Bar-Tal who led the audit. 'But when we talk about textbooks, all the children, all of a particular peer group, will be exposed to a particular material,' he added. 'This is the strongest card.'

Qasim Aslam, co-founder of The History Project, agrees about the potency of what he calls 'hatred content' in text books, whether they are produced in his native Pakistan or over the border by traditional rivals, India. 'Very few people on either side would argue History is taught correctly, that it is a 'set of facts' the teachers are presenting. But they are not optimistic they can do much about it – or solve this at scale – especially as governments ultimately call the shots and it's an intensely political issue.'

Qasim, a young leader I met through the Seeds of Peace initiative (SoP), decided to do something about it. SoP is a peace-making venture set up by the Clinton Administration in the wake of the Oslo Accords that brings together young people from conflict areas (initially the

Middle East, but now including the sub-continent and beyond) so they can learn how to heal their differences and find common ground.

'I'll never forget a session at the SoP camp', recounts Qasim, 'when all the so-called enemies were brought together and we were encouraged to discuss our histories. I thought it was going to be a back-to-school type session and wasn't enthusiastic, but when I got into that room it all changed. As we compared 'facts', it was clear the very same incidents have been reported on different sides from completely different perspectives and with very extreme language. The contrast was so stark it made us all realise, there's something wrong here.'

The History Project is now triggering similar awakenings in young students all over the sub-continent by placing starkly contrasting 'factual' textbook accounts of the same events side-by-side in the same publication and letting students figure out that *something is wrong*.

One startling visual Qasim and his team use to great effect shows Ghandi, peace-loving, unifying Father of the Nation as the Indians see him, alongside the blindfolded, cynical statesman turning his back on Muslim interests that Pakistanis are brought up to recognise as the 'real' Mahatma.

Another example of dissonant, parallel histories that Qasim draws my attention to is the so-called Lahore Resolution. Pakistani students are taught this is the momentous day in 1940 when the Muslim League, led by Muhammad Ali Jinnah, Pakistan's founder, passed the motion to set up a separate Muslim state, an Islamic homeland independent of India. Indian students are also taught about the Lahore Resolution. But theirs refers to the midnight of New Year's 1929 when India's President, Jawaharlal Nehru, symbolically placed the tricolour of India on the banks of the river Ravi in Lahore, signifying the independence of India – a unified Hindu-Muslim India – from Britain.

Two completely different resolutions – with diametrically opposed implications – but *exactly the same* name. This kind of confusion, as the future hackers are perfectly well aware, is a recipe for discord.

Qasim, his partner Ayyaz and their team of young leaders are doing their part to challenge this kind of wilful future hack. But it requires a light touch. Or they could be accused of adding their own voice to the mayhem. 'We don't tell students what to think. We are not putting in our own ideas of history, of who is right or wrong. We just want kids to start asking questions.'

As The History Project's site powerfully puts it:

More than two billion young impressionable minds learn history through textbooks. The narratives are often biased and always from a single perspective, contributing to the intolerant world that we live in today.

If you want to see how a group of young leaders are using story to counter intolerance and promote peace, I'd highly recommend you visit the site (www.seeds ofpeace.org). And if you happen to be a school or university teacher anywhere in the world reading this, you'll also be able to download valuable tools to help seed more healthy narratives in the classroom.

Our culture does it ...

Our cultures are bursting with ideas and expectations about what is and is not an acceptable future. Take gender, for example, and how our culture tends to plot quite different paths for men and women.

Yes, we've come quite a way since the woman was chained to the stove making dinner for the bread-winning male. But there's still a huge amount of work to do. Sheryl Sandberg's *Lean In* cites a prominent children's clothing company who, as recently as 2010, was selling two romper suits for toddlers: a blue one with the slogan 'smart like daddy' and a pink one with 'pretty like mommy'.

Whether we are aware of it or not, cultural norms shape what we think we can accomplish, our likely life partner(s), how many children we will or won't have, our life expectancy.

If you think it's far-fetched that culture can affect something as life and death as death, consider 'the pointing of the bone', a ritual death sentence traditionally practised by certain Aboriginal tribes in central and northern Australia. Essentially what happens is this. The tribal executioner (the *Kaditcha*) arrives on the guilty party's doorstep wearing feathered shoes and carrying the femur of an emu or kangaroo. He points the fatal bone and the condemned person dies, usually within a couple of weeks. There are scientific reasons for this. There's a well-documented phenomenon called 'voodoo death' or 'psychogenic death' where the body loses the will to live and succumbs to fatal torpor and/or terrifies itself to the grave through what the doctors have identified as 'parasympathetic overstimulation' of the fear and stress response. But essentially people drop dead after having been cursed in a bone-pointing because their culture says they will. It's a self-fulfilling prophecy.

It's nowhere near as extreme – and a long way from the outback – but there is growing evidence of a connection between being 'retired' and being 'dead'. Retirement is a relatively new idea. Before the 20th century most people just worked until they fell off their perch. In 1880s Britain, for example, 78% of men over the age of 65 were still working.

The advent of a pension system and a welfare state gave rise to the notion of retirement, a period of time when the hardworking citizen could enjoy leisure before death. Unfortunately, humans, especially males of the species, rely on work to support their identity and, by extension, their emotional health. Extended leisure removes this connection, makes them feel useless and they duly die. Yes, there are additional medical reasons that account for the correlation between early retirement and early death – but cultural expectation is clearly an important factor.

So, there it is. We have been comprehensively Future Hacked! Thanks to the combined efforts of family, education, society, media, politics, commerce and culture.

And the cost?

We are all to a greater or lesser extent living someone else's version of our future rather than our own.

It may be fine to live someone else's future. But I'd argue you'll be more successful, become a better leader, have more fun, experience more freedom, come up with better ideas, work more creatively, have more impact, enjoy life and laugh more if you author your own.

You've got all the techniques I've shared up to now in this book for writing and telling a story. Now it's time to apply them to something really important. Your life. Putting together a narrative that doesn't just describe the world – but changes it.

This may not appeal. It may seem fanciful. You may opt instead to return here to the real world and continue living as 'reality' demands. That's fine, just remember what you are choosing is not *real*, it's fiction – one that someone else cooked up for you.

So, yes this a threshold moment. A red pill/blue pill choice point, for lovers of the *Matrix*. There's no necessity to say yes. But you'll be rewarded with adventures if you do. I'm going to look away now and if this isn't for you, just close the book. Thanks, it's been real.

Otherwise step over the dotted line and let's have some fun with the future …

● ● ● ● ● ●

AUTHORING THE FUTURE

 You can use story to describe what's happening. Or you can go further and use it to invent what you want to happen! Start looking at the future as an author. Here are some tips about how to do this. Then, pick up your pen and start …

Chapter 7

AUTHORING THE FUTURE

Welcome. Glad you made it. This is the real reason I wrote this book. It's the stuff that most interests me – that I am most passionate to research.

It's about how we overwrite these compelling futures that others have planned for us and create our own.

Draw up a chair, grab a glass of water (this work requires you stay well hydrated) and make yourself a little bit *un*comfortable. Future Authoring isn't always relaxing – and you are going to spend quite a bit of time on the edge of your seat.

We're going to swivel the comfortable, review-mirror formula of '*Once upon a time there was …*' to the rather less familiar thinking of '*Once upon a time, there will be …*'

Now, how you author your future is up to you. I am going to suggest some steps that will get you going and enable you to apply what you've learned so far. It'll be a great chance for you to review the previous chapters with application in mind. And a chance for me to check if you've been listening to a word I said!

I'll also suggest some principles to keep in mind. I am going to mix these up so you won't know exactly what's coming. As I say, no-one can write your story for you, but I will do my best to provoke you and make the journey enjoyable.

Take authority

The first step is actually a pre-first step; a step zero. It's a mindset you need to have before you can do any future authoring.

You can think of it as *taking authority*.

Interesting word, authority. Especially for a leader. It derives from the Latin *auctor*, literally 'originator or promoter' and came to mean in Middle English 'some-one who invents or causes something'. Long before it was associated with writing, or creativity, authorship re-ferred to an essential quality of leadership: the ability to create.

No one is going to give you authority to create your future. They are too interested in you living their version. You have to take authority yourself and it begins with a simple declaration:

I have the right to make up the future!

Try it. Don't be put off by the mental chattering as ghostly teachers, parents, politicians, pundits and the rest fight back … *You're crazy … You can't do without us … It's been tried before … You're deluding yourself … Stay home … Who are you to break the rules, you're only six years old!*

Don't be put off. Tell yourself. *I give myself permission. I am allowed.*

Once you're (more or less) comfortable with this idea, once you've authorised yourself to create what's coming, you have a metaphorical blank sheet in front of you. It's not a planning sheet or a To Do list. It's the snowy white background for you to scribe a future story.

Wonderful. And a little bit terrifying.[1]

If you are saying to yourself: 'I have never done this before!' Strictly speaking that's not true. You have been fictionalising and story making your entire life. Remember, almost everything in your mind right now didn't happen, isn't happening and/or won't happen. We are Homo *fictionalis*. This is what we do. We pretend for a living.

---

[1] I've done this a lot and honestly it's still not comfortable. Actually, I think if the first act of authorship doesn't make your tum turn over just a little, you probably aren't doing it right.

Your story in a sentence

What do you want your future story to be about? Remember, an author can write what they *want* not what they *should*. Keep it really simple. Most good stories can be summarised in a few words:

> *Boy wizard and his two friends battle to prevent Dark Lord taking over the world.*

Or

> *Independently-minded young lady falls in love with a wealthy aristocrat when she overcomes her pride, and he his prejudices.*

Or

> *Plucky student criminologist traps serial killer by enrolling the help of another serial killer.*

The basic formula is that person A does action B despite obstacle C and earns reward D.

Or to be even more simple: an ordinary person does something extraordinary. Give it a go!

_____

_____

_____

_____

Perfectionism alert!

Well done. Bet that wasn't easy. Committing yourself to paper like that.

One of the reasons most novels-to-be stay unwritten and the screenplay you dream about doesn't make it to the screen is the part of you – we all have one – that thinks *I have to get this right!*

It's the voice of judgement, the inner critic that thinks it knows what *right* is and won't accept anything less from you. Judgement is the enemy of the creative process and this mental know-all will blight your future story if you let it. Two antidotes?

1. *Start simply*. We just did that.
2. *Simply start*. There's nothing more liberating that just writing something. Anything. Rubbish if it has to be. You can always change, edit, rewrite later.

Perfectionism is also often the root cause of the dreaded Writer's Block. We can't write because everything that comes to mind seems inadequate. Speaking for myself, I want you to love this book. Adore it, actually. But if that is my baseline – if I won't commit anything to page that doesn't meet that exacting (and impossible) standard, I wouldn't get a line down on paper.

If Writer's Block should strike you at any time in this process, I would pass on the helpful advice one writer gave me: 'If you get stuck, lower your standards.'

Real writers are rewriters

Another reason you can relax your way into this is because you have a luxury most deny ourselves in the rest of life: drafting and redrafting.

When I first started working in business I was amazed by how little time people spent refining. Half a day at a flip chart was considered more than enough time to devise a grand new vision. Five minutes to create five bullet points for five years? Bags of time. Never has so much been risked by so many people on ideas that have had so few minutes spent on them.

Get it right, and move on is the business mantra.

One thing my time in the arts has taught me is there is no right. There's an original idea. And then there's constant refining. Movies never get finished, goes the old saying. You just run out of time. And/or money.

The great news about authoring the future is it costs nothing and you have the whole of the rest of your life to work on it. This is an iterative process where your ongoing experience continually informs the unfolding story.

Perhaps I can my use my own evolving story as an example. When I started this work over 20 years ago I would have told you my 'why', my inner verb, the underlying motor of the story, was to 'kindle the being in others'. Sounds a bit airy fairy, I know, but I was deeply into some quite esoteric work at the time. That language resonated for me and was right for then. I kept refining, and a while later my 'why' had morphed into the simple 'to inspire'. More specifically 'to help organisations become more inspired and inspiring'. This served well, until one day, when I was tinkling the piano, a new 'why' knocked its predecessor off its perch (and me off my piano stool – literally). My 'why', went the author in my head, 'is that everyone lives their why.' That is still serving me well but I have a hunch it is about to be replaced again with the latest iteration.

So, why don't you rewrite your story in a sentence? And let's see if we can improve it.

_____

_____

_____

_____

_____

_____

_____

_____

_____

_____

It may already have got better without my attempts at helpful guidance. A few pages is plenty of time for the mind to come up with a new, improved draft. Even better, leave it overnight and think about it in the morning. It's what I call the Sock Drawer Principle. All teenage boys will know this. Leave smelly socks (or underwear) in a drawer for long enough and they will cure themselves.

Here are a couple of ways you might want to improve things.

1. Write about yourself in third person

When you describe yourself in this story summary, do it as he or she, not I. This helps you to step out of your skin, to step aside from the everyday you and take a fresh perspective. You are the author of this story, yes, but also a character in it.

It could be you (*plucky mid-life professional, working mum, student at start of career, outwardly successful but confused leader, friend to everyone but themselves*). Or it could be your organisation (*sleeping giant, plucky start up, committed NGO, UK concern with international dreams, much loved local store, undiscovered treasure of a printing works*). It could also be your family, community, even country.

2. Choose a good verb

This doesn't have to be detailed. Just choose something strong and vivid. *Overcomes difficulties? Discovers the truth? Fights for freedom? Finds true love? Makes an indelible mark on history?* I wouldn't recommend anything too woolly (comes to terms with man's essential meaninglessness – leave that to French novels). Nor anything too mundane. If the heart of your story is 'reorganises the stockroom', I for one won't be watching to see how it turns out.

Bearing those points in mind, try another draft below. And while you are at it, I will do the same.

_____

_____

_____

_____

_____

_____

_____

_____

_____

_____

_____

Here's what I came up with.

A professional future story:

> *A gifted but easily distracted creative stops avoiding his vocation and so finds true fulfilment.*

A business future story:

> *A small but high potential business moves from flight to space travel by embracing its true nature.*

A personal future story:

> *In the wake of his father's death a son learns how*
> *to make every day count for the rest of his life.*

Now write your own review

Today we are all reviewers. App raters. Trip advisors. Everyone seems to want to know our opinions on products, films, restaurants, blog posts. So why not jump right to the end of the story you are authoring and give it a review right now. What would you like the review to say about your future story? About the content, the experience, the level of excitement and satisfaction? Here's an example from a young woman in a Life Scripting session with me a few years back:

> *A sweet love story in a hard corporate world.*
> *A romantic journey you will never forget. Two*
> *people with a non-stop lifestyle set off to*
> *enjoy the world and each other. This excellently*
> *written book offers an escape from the ordinary*
> *life and makes you feel happy and fall asleep*
> *with a smile on your face; it's what life is*
> *about!*

And this is a review about a story yet to be written, remember. Yet to be lived. The future author here was a fast-tracker in a professional services firm. You can sense there are difficulties in her life. Work-life imbalances. Doubts about the world she is working in.

But there's real clarity about the story she intends to write, the kind of humanised career she wants to have and the positive effect she intends this story to have on others.

She didn't know how to get to the future exactly, so I asked her to jump to the future, look back and figure out what it is going to take to get her there.

That's what I am asking you to do now.

So write your review.

_____

_____

_____

_____

_____

_____

_____

_____

_____

_____

And, heck, why not give it a rating as well. One to five stars.

You and who else?

Dorothy didn't make it to Oz alone. Luke Skywalker only blew up the Death Star with help. One Samurai needs six others to beat the bad guys. The Magnificent One doesn't really cut it. Do you really see Oceans 3 breaking the Bellagio? Tony Soprano cannot sing alone. And Band of Brother – is just sad.

You get the point. The key to a great story is a great cast of characters. The future story you are authoring now is no exception.

Typical people you might want to weave in are:

- Love interest
- Faithful side-kick
- Wise guide (Morgan Freeman has cornered the market in these)

I mean this quite literally. Go cast them. Approach people in your life that you want to feature in your future story and ask them to be in your cast of characters. Chances are they will be really honoured.

Even when you are not authoring the future, you'll find it a powerful way as a leader to assemble your team.

Do include naysayers, cynical bystanders and frustrator figures.

And don't forget You Know Who ...

Every story has one. They featured in all of your past stories. And the future you are authoring is full of them. They're the worthy adversaries, the obstacle creators. They're your nemesis. And they are also the fuel to power your story.

Think, right now, what you are up against. What stands between you and what you want? Who shows up as a foe, ally…? It doesn't have to be a 'who' it can be a 'what'. You can create a great story where you are up against TIME. There's a pressing thing you need to do but you have to do it against the clock. There are those who say that's the planet's current story.

Choose a genre

What type of story do you want to be living over the next X years? We'll come to the time scale in a minute. Where would the story of your future sit in the bookshelves of a high street store? In which category of Netflix do you want the film of this book to be found?

Is it going to be an action story? Or a drama? Or a romance? A triumph against the odds tale? A coming of age fable, or a rite of passage?

Or what about combining genres into sub genres? A romantic action drama, perhaps. A boy-meets-girl-meets-historical comedy with sci-fi twist?

It's fun to play genre bingo. But choosing a genre has genuine value when you are authoring your future. It's your way of identifying the qualities you want your future story – that is to say, your future – to have.

Maybe it's time to bring some thriller quality into your working life. Or mystery into your domestic narrative. When my wife and I moved our family back to London from the Italian countryside in 2011 we looked at each other and deliberately asked how we were going to make the next years, back in our familiar 'hood', as much of an adventure as the story we had been living.

A word of caution. You may be tempted to make your future story something of a comedy. Comedies, you have to know, are hugely enjoyable to watch but intensely uncomfortable to live. It is actually the discomfort of the protagonists that causes us to laugh.

Time and a place

When do you want your future tale to unfold?

_____

And where?

_____

A fundamental choice this; it sets the scale and scope of your narrative. It could unfold in your back garden or span the globe. Or beyond. Steve Jobs, remember, talked about making a ding in the universe.

A good way to focus your scope is decide if your story is about ...

My World? – affecting you and those immediately connected to you.

Or

Our World? – involving your wider community.

Or

The World? – having visible impact on Earth, the sort you'd see from space.

And how long from beginning to end? What's your time horizon? I believe it was Anthony Robbins (he of the great height, unfeasibly white teeth and undeniable brilliance) that said: 'We overestimate what we can do in one year and underestimate what we can do in ten.'

Five years is a good guide. I'd say no less than three. It generally takes a couple of years to make any significant progress. And if you want to take the story to the end of your life, that's great, just remember the age you 'think' you will die is only a story – probably someone else's.

Step back, put your head on one side and get some perspective on perspective[2]

When things are going wrong in the businesses I serve, when people are overstressed, or things seem especially dark, when personal survival trumps collective responsibility, when bosses set undo-able targets and browbeaten teams pay lip service to them – it's time to reset perspective.

Perspective changes everything.

When you set out to *create* perspective – in your story

---

2 *Everything we hear is an opinion, not a fact. Everything we see is a perspective, not the truth* (Marcus Aurelius).

or in your workplace – you have two principal co-ordinates/axes/levers to play with. One is TIME. The other is PLACE.

Musk has created a story that ends on Mars in his life-time. That's a crucial part of the excitement. If he said, one day we'll migrate to Mars, we'd turn the page. But he intends to get there in 20 years. Yes, you heard right. As *The Guardian* reports in a recent interview:

> *Musk's belief that this can be achieved in two decades is something that most experts would scoff at but Musk, characteristically, finds it frustratingly slow. 'Twenty years seems like semi-infinity to me. That's a long time,' he says, as if surprised that anyone could doubt his aims. It is certainly tempting to dismiss it as a flight of fancy. Except, behind him on SpaceX's factory floor, Musk's nascent fleet of working space rockets are already being built.*

By choosing a 20 year, rather than 200 year perspective, Musk generates real energy and excitement. Calling two decades a 'semi-infinity' is deliberately provocative to the 'experts'. But it's clearly deliberate. By creating an energising perspective for his story, he wakes people up to new possibilities and makes everyone around him – an entire industry – accelerate their expectations.

I've seen firsthand how galvanising it can be to shift

a team's time perspective. Like it or loathe it, no one can argue with the speed and ambition of Dubai's recent growth. Barely more than a community of traders and fishermen in the 1950s, the city state has exploded into one of the most eye-poppingly futuristic destinations on Earth.

Working with some of the region's visionaries, I conclude that one of the reasons they can achieve what, to us, seems implausible is that they don't see time as we do. I have been a fly on the wall in some interesting meetings where the Emirates most successful and impatient developers halved the completion time of a huge new development. 'I know it should take 20 years, but it needs to take 10 as I want to enjoy it while I am still alive.'

'Rome wasn't built in a day' say the more moderate heads, 'these things take time'. The Dubai rule is different. Things take the time you are prepared to tolerate them taking. You set the timeline and let reality reorganise itself.

A client of mine, a hugely impressive and major player in Dubai's property boom, confided that the Emir is hard to keep up with. Last month a journalist asked him how much of his vision has been realised to date and High Highness responded 'four percent'. Last week another journalist asked the same question and he said 'three percent'. 'But last month you said four percent, Your Highness' … 'Yes, but my vision just got bigger'.

This is a part of the world where they are not planning their future, they are inventing it.

Imagine applying that same entrepreneurial itchiness to resolving climate change. Or social strife. Or... Or our own plans and visions? How would our own lives differ if we altered our time perspective and gave ourselves less time?

Think about the time perspective you are setting yourself. Whether you realise it or not, you do have one. Take a look back at the line of your life. I asked you to draw the line of your life – past, present and future – and mark with an X where you are. Well, where did you place the X? Most of the business people I have done this with – and that's thousands – place their X somewhere around the middle; usually, if it's a professional, middle-aged audience, 4/7ths of the way along the line. It's a simple way of revealing to ourselves the unconscious time perspective that's running in the background of our lives. The X says *I have 3/7ths of my life left* or 50% or whatever. The question is, how do you know? You may be right. And I hope your life lasts just as long as you want it to. That said, our assessment of the time we have left is guesswork – at best. What if your guess is wrong? And how would you live your life differently if the end point of your life story were actually different. Especially if it was much closer.

Some of the most successful, creative, appreciative and stimulating people I have ever met live as though their end could be closer than they are planning. Hope for a long life, but shorten their expectations just in case. They don't sit back in a nice comfy 'I've got plenty of time' lassitude. They up the tempo, squeeze life out of every day. They are conscious of their time perspective and authorial about where they place it.

The opposite is true. Over-shortening your time perspective can be the most debilitating and stress making thing you can do to yourself – or allow others to do to you. *There's not enough time* is the lament of the modern workplace. How much stress and pain is generated by collapsing timescales so they are too close, too busy, too full. How many night's sleep are being interrupted, how much alcohol chugged, pills popped and cigarettes furtively puffed by people telling themselves there's too much to do and too little time to do it?

I'd go further and say there's always an unhelpful, if unconscious, time perspective operating when we are going through a hard time or experiencing mental suffering.

- Broken hearted: 'I'll never love/be loved like that again.'
- Regret: 'It's too late/too soon.'
- Despair: 'The way I feel will last forever!'
- Self-doubt: 'I'm too old/young to…'

I say this as someone who has had my own experience of depression earlier in life. One of the most dispiriting and alarming aspects of that condition is the way that time seems to disappear; you feel like the horrible way you feel now is going to last for eternity.

The leader that's authoring the future knows that shifting time perspective can turn things around.

The second coordinate which the leader uses to create a compelling perspective for their story is space.

Elon Musk isn't going to Manchester. Or the Maldives. Or even the Moon. He is going to Mars. The canvas he has chosen – the context he and his colleagues are working within – is epic, interplanetary. What this context gives is meaning.

When an organisation or team has lost its way, a smart leader will reposition their efforts relative to the rest of the industry. If they are complacent, she will remind them the competition is closing. When they become self-obsessed or too inward looking, the leader shifts their attention to the wider world.

I am struck by how perplexed many businesses are to be experiencing exponential change. And how this stress eases when they recognise they are not alone and that out there – yes look out there – exponential change is something *every* company is experiencing.

When people are feeling lost – and it can easily happen in any organisation – perspective literally explains *where we are* right now.

Spatial perspective is also about creating a sequence so your audience understands *where we were* and *where we are heading next.*

One evening I was sitting at a kitchen table having dinner with the CEO of a pioneering online bank. He had a lot on his mind; awkward dilemmas, contradictory advice, shareholder pressure, too many options, too little time to consider them and lots of free-floating stress. Publicly, he comes across as something of a financial Titan. But here, after hours, when the mask was down, he had the look of a man who wasn't sure exactly where he was, how he had got here and where to go next. You or I would probably have felt the same in his position.

On an impulse I lined up the bottles of tomato sauce, olive oil, balsamic vinegar with some cutlery and a few stray bread rolls into what the business world calls a timeline. I prefer to think of it as a storyline, and a particularly powerful one.

I pointed out the three main phases (beginning, middle and end), the highs and lows and the thresholds between. Then I asked Paul: 'If this is your story – where are you right now?'

He pointed to a low point between the saltcellar and the serviette ring. 'Here's where I am and…' there was a long pause as Paul took in the whole vista. The whole uneasy process of his business adventure was laid out on a messy tablecloth.

'And… here's where we go next.' Unstuck, he was off.

Suddenly Paul had a map. Now there was a

logic to the otherwise disconnected events of recent months, which helped him understand and accept his current situation. Looking back he could see how much he was the author of what had happened. Looking down the storyline he could see new phases awaited. And most importantly, he could now get really creative about the story he wanted to author in the future.

I said there are two axes to perspective, but there's a third you might find useful, not just in your future *neurative*, but in all aspects of daily life. I call it Altitude Control. As a future author you can see the world from close up, helicopter view or from way up in space. You can zoom in and out as you like … micro detail, or broad sweep.

Give your future story a title

That love story in the corporate world was called *Join the Dots* by the way. Choose one for your own future story. One that would encourage you to take it off the shelf in Waterstones, click it on Amazon, buy it on Net-flix.

It could be a title which intrigues, which amuses, which paints a mind picture.[3]

---

[3] Or sound track. If I were Elon Musk's publisher I'd probably suggest *Life on Mars* not least because it would trigger your mind to play the Bowie song.

Examples from the same Author the Future workshop include:

- *The Night the World Stopped Turning*
- *Shout it Out*
- *Go for It*
- *A Life on the Rocks* (the writer was a rock guitarist)
- *Hey Wanderlamp* (no, me neither)

So, what will yours be?

True AND false

This is going to sound odd, but as an author of the future, your story needs to be both true *and* false: real *and* unreal.

I'll explain.

But first, test how your drafts are shaping up by reading your story aloud. Ideally looking at yourself in a mirror.

If the story sounds reasonable, keep working. Who wants a reasonable future story? You want one which makes you smile. Or makes you feel queasy with excitement. It might even make you laugh out loud it's so implausible. The root of that laughter is what psychologists call 'cognitive dissonance' – the stress that's created when the mind's desire to create consistency between beliefs and reality is violated.

In normal life, the unsettled mind will often deny,

denigrate or dismiss the implausible idea. When you are a leader in authoring the future mode, that disbelieving laughter is a sign you are on the right track.

Land a man on the moon? Votes for women? Affordable healthcare for all? Information split into bytes, travelling the globe via a world wide web, and reconstituting itself on your computer screen? ... You have GOT TO BE KIDDING!!!

Cognitive Dissonance might freak your brain out, but it's the leader's friend. It's your way of awakening the sleepy people around you to what's possible. Then you can start to make the implausible fiction a reality.

Because it is not yet realised, your future story will, by definition, seem unreal. It cannot agree with the stories the future hackers have installed in your mental hard drive. It has to be false, if you like.

But if you are going to overwrite other people's stories, displace them with your own, you have to make them seem very very real. Our minds don't know the difference between reality and a deeply imagined fiction. You need to make the future model you are describing so three-dimensional that people can imagine themselves already there. Which is why it's important you use vivid, sensory, emotional language – the language of *story* not *planning* – to describe it.

Leaders create futures and then work back from them. They know how to install a compelling future into the minds of those they lead. And if the fiction is compelling enough, those minds will set about making the story real.

The title, the review, the vivid verbs, the rich adjectives – they all help make your story real for the processors in your cerebral cortex. That's why I often think of future stories as Neuratives not Narratives.

You DO know what's coming!

So have confidence.

This is a key component of authority. It's also one of the joys of being an author. You do know what comes next because you are making it up! It's not based on evidence. It doesn't have to be reasonable. It's just what you say it is.

And don't let any consultant or expert tell you, you don't. The detail, perhaps not. But the elements? You know there will be ups and downs. You know there are going to be risks to face and tricky choices to make. And you know that the future will surprise you.

You know this. So do the people you lead, by the way. That's why, when you are waxing on about a great new idea, they are not beaming back. They know the way ahead is far different from what you are describing in the PowerPoint or the business plan. Hidden behind that arrow straight line from today to the realisation of your new vision, there's another line. The life line. And it's a roller coaster.

We know what's coming next because of our past

experience. It tends to be circular, with familiar experiences reoccurring. We know from history which tends to repeat itself (*first as tragedy and second as farce*, according to Karl Marx).

But we most particularly know what's coming because other authors have been telling you for centuries. We know stories evolved so we could learn in safety about what lies ahead. And through the ages, story makers have been giving us a heads-up about what's likely to happen any time you set out to do something different.

Remember this as we get to…

The wobbly bit …

Ask anyone from the literature professor to the preschoolers and they will tell you stories have essentially three bits.

You could describe them as beginning, middle and end.

I prefer to think of them as beginning – WHOAH WHAT THE BLEEP IS GOING ON I DON'T KNOW WHAT'S COMING NEXT OR WHERE I AM GOING IT'S EXCITING BUT I'D RATHER BE ON TERRA FIRMA THAN OUT HERE WHERE IT'S ALL DIFFERENT AND WHAT I HAVE LEARNED SO FAR DOESN'T HELP ME AND WHY DID I EVEN THINK ABOUT STARTING THIS BUT NOW I HAVE I HAD BETTER PLOUGH ON AND DO WHAT I SET OUT TO DO EVEN THOUGH I SERIOUSLY DOUBT I AM CAPABLE OF IT – end.

It's the wobbly bit. The bit in between the opening status quo and our final landing. It is where the energy of the story lies. Nobody queues in the rain to see a story where things move smoothly from A–Z. It's the switch-back ride that makes the story worth telling.

So while you will be tempted to smooth out the likely bumps as you are authoring your future story – I strongly urge you not to. I'd actually make that bucking storyline even more dynamic.

A great way to do this, to keep your characters (including you) developing, learning, problem solving, growing, is by weaving in 'moments of truth'. These are essentially situations which force you and those with you to make choices. You can make default choices. If you do, your future story will look a lot like your past one. Or you could use the moment of truth to choose something different, to stretch, to reach beyond, to go against the grain and enjoy the unexpected consequences.

Here are my top ten moments of truth that I have culled from world literature and film.

1. The call

This is a moment, it may already have happened while working on your story, when the universe calls your bluff. Shortly after you get clear about your story and what it is you want to experience/achieve/contribute/enjoy, life has a way of sending exactly that opportunity your way. It's known in the story literature as 'the call to adventure'. It doesn't always call though. It can whisper. The question is will the protagonist – you – spot it? And once you do, what then?

2. The dither

This is an important moment of truth that comes just after the call. Academics call it the 'refusal of the call'. It's the moment when you – when we all – dodge and fudge. Life sends us an invitation to party and instead of RSVP-ing we tuck the invite behind the kettle and say we'll get round to it later. It's only cartoon characters that dash into action. The rest of us hedge. And we have done since stories have been told. We know to Err is Human. Turns out to Errrrrr is Human too.

3. Should I stay or should I go?

So there you are, hovering at the boundary between the known and the unknown. We know you are going to cross *the threshold* as scholars sonorously describe it. The question is how? Are you going to be pushed – by circumstances, time running out, burning platforms? Or are you going to be pulled – galvanised to take the big step by excitement and curiosity about what the future holds? There is a third way and it's the most common for us flesh and blood humans. We stumble across, like we've tried to stride but forgot our shoe-laces are tied together.

4. The push back

OK, so you've tripped over the threshold to the future on your bold mission and the first thing you meet is – resistance. Stories, especially the wobbly bits, are not hospitable places for their main characters. What makes this a moment of truth is how you respond when the world says 'you're crazy'.

5. The tough choice

We write the difficulties in, remember. And nothing is more difficult than making choices. Action takes muscle. Choices take spirit. A good story – and yours is going to be a cracker, I am sure – will test you by forcing you to make choices you would rather avoid. These choices show us who you really are. As TS Eliot says: 'If you are not in over your head, how do you know how tall you are?'

6. The impossible choice

There are tough choices – which force you to choose be-tween right and wrong. You encounter these every day. You can get these wrong but at least there is a correct answer. What every good story does – at least once – is force their main character to tackle a *dilemma*. A dilemma forces you to make a choice not between right and wrong, but between right and right – or wrong and wrong. Dilemmas can't be figured out, they have to be felt through. You don't need data, you need leadership and courage. Indeed, they are the mark of leadership and courage. That's why writers put them in stories. Right now you have a good idea about some of the dilemmas that could lie ahead in your future story. You're probably avoiding them. Don't. Write the dilemmas IN.

7. Save yourselves

About two thirds of the way along the storyline, a good writer will make things so challenging for their main character(s) they will be tempted to give up. It's the dark night of the soul. The moment where the faltering hero tells us 'leave me here and save yourselves'. Does the writer leave the hero out there to expire in the tundra/jungle, to pine away for love, to be beaten by the system, to accept compromise and defeat? Hell, no. In the depths of that low point, the main character will usually have a crucial breakthrough. They'll accept some wisdom they have been denying. Peer beyond their habitual blind spot. Like finding a crucial lost part of the story jigsaw that's been hidden under the narrative sofa. And that transforms the low point into a turning point, a spring board that bounces the story arc upwards towards the next high. Low points are much more helpful than high ones. They teach you more.

8. The rumble

Here's where you finally face the nemesis and duke it out. It's also known as the Supreme Test or Trial. This is the moment when you get to look your fear right in the eyes – and see who blinks first. WE love this moment in stories. And avoid it at all costs in life. That's one reason stories exist, so we can explore potentially explosive confrontation vicariously and in safety.

9. The romantic rumble

The climactic encounter doesn't have to be one person conquering another. It can be about love conquering all. It's the moment after 90 minutes of dithering that the hero or heroine crosses the yawning space that has been separating them from their love interest – and kisses them. It can be every bit as daunting as the violent rumble. And will often lead to rough and tumble.

10. The reunion

So, with luck, you emerge from the sparks and smoke of the big encounter older, wiser, enriched by your experience. You have a tale to tell and you return home (or wherever your starting point was) to tell it. This is the reward and return element of the hero's journey myth. Trouble is, when you are reunited with your past life, it often doesn't recognise you, appreciate your wisdom or even trust you anymore. Which is why I think of this as the reunion moment – as in school reunion. An event which promises much but is usually disorientating (why have they aged while I have stayed the same) and something of an anticlimax.

The anticlimax is intentional by the way – a deliberate cool down period that takes you from the peak of the story towards the ending.

Which is where we are heading right now.

THE END?

 We generally don't like to think about endings. Endings mean change and change is threatening. In life and business. Knowing where and how the story ends is an essential element of authoring the future. And of leadership.

Chapter 7

THE END?

I am always intrigued when people describe themselves as 'middle aged'. How do they know they are in the middle? Why not a third of the way through life? Or nine-tenths? There are people who woke up this morning who won't wake up tomorrow. And most of them will be surprised by this.

We make assumptions about our lifeline and how far we have travelled along it. We know it's a guess but we tend to leave it at that because it's unsettling to dwell on the big E.

Generally, we don't want things to end. There are some exceptions, of course. Brian's interminable presentation about the new health and safety regulations? Let it end! That cold call from the contact centre in Mysore which

rings just as dinner hits the table. *Let it En*d. Haemor-
rhoid pain and/or Justin Bieber songs? *Let it END!*

But things like delicious meals, wonderful holidays,
fulfilling relationships, great sex, lucky breaks, winning
streaks, exciting projects, our own success, careers, companies and – yes – our own lives? We'd rather they
continued. Forever. Preferably, getting better all the time.

It's funny. We know we won't live forever, but we
don't act as though we know.

Just look at how we, as a race, have an infinite
appetite for the planet's finite resources. And how eco-
nomically we're building up debts we know we can't pay
back. What previous more savings-minded generations
called *living on the never-never.*

One sure sign that people are living like they'll never
die is – boredom.

I realised this in an unlikely place, the top of a sweaty
London bus, stuck in a traffic jam on a cold November
evening a few years ago. I was frustrated not to be home.
I was irritated by my fellow travellers. They were noisy,
smelly and standing too near me. I am nearly two metres
tall and the top deck of a bus isn't. So I was physically
uncomfortable too. Moan, moan, moan.

Suddenly my mind asked me an unexpected question:
'*Imagine you were dead and you were given the chance
to come back to life for a minute. But there's a catch.
That minute has to be spent here – on this crowded,
smelly, grid-locked bus.*' Would you take that minute of

extra life? Absolutely. And would you be bored? Absolutely not! I bet I'd spend that minute marvelling at life, drinking in the details, appreciating the privilege of having a body at all, savouring the sweaty proximity of the other passengers, enjoying the pure magic of being alive. That was the day I realised the only reason we ever get bored is because we think we'll live forever. Moaning is for immortals.

I suppose it's understandable. Finality means change. And change tends to make humans uneasy. We know things have to end – we have to end – but we don't like to think about how or when.

Authors, on the other hand, love to think about The End. They know a great ending is second only to a great beginning – that even a compelling tale can be let down by an anticlimactic close. Great stories can't fade away, they have to go out with a bang, not a whimper.

In this final chapter – sorry, spoiler alert, like everything else, this book is coming to its end – I thought we could spend our last minutes together looking at endings and some powerful ways to think about them. I think you'll find these useful, both when you are future authoring and in your day-to-day leadership.

Keep endings in mind

Remember how your parents always seemed to know where they were driving you on holiday – even when they were clearly lost? As a leader who is authoring the future you need to be the same. Your team is probably not made up of children and you're unlikely to be driving in the dark looking for a hotel that the map says should be there. But you need to radiate a confidence about where you are going.

That means being clear about the final destination (*the Promised Land that is being promised*) and set a decisive direction (*it's that way …*) knowing you may have to course-correct later on.

What you *don't* need to do is print an itemised itinerary. The journey to the future is not a commute with neatly mapped out bus and metro stops. You don't have to know exactly how you get where you are going. You don't actually want to – where's the fun in that? The detail will emerge over time.

End frequently. End well

A well-crafted story doesn't have one ending. If you look closely, there are mini and micro-endings throughout. Each act, each chapter, even each sentence has its own full stop. A leader both notes these and celebrates them.

If the end point of your future narrative is distant, you need to treat each step towards the goal as a mini story of its own. That's a lesson I learned working with the long-sighted scientists at GSK Vaccines.

Vaccine development is a notoriously drawn out business. Researching a new product, developing and testing it, then finally bringing it to market can take more than a decade. Some of my clients were working on vaccines that wouldn't be released until after they had retired. What kept them going was the small victories, the annual progress, the monthly inching forward.

The most effective leaders were those that recognised these mini-chapters and celebrated their conclusion.

Celebrate endings

Celebration is a wonderful way of marking an ending by the way. I say this because it is SO RARE in the businesses I have served. In most cases you hardly know when one piece of work ends and another begins. Projects blur into each other. The passing of quarters are marked with earnings reports at best. And soon one year seems much like any other.

Celebrating the ends of even small things is smart. When you mark the end of something, you generate energy for the next phase. Our ancestors knew this. Think of the harvest festivals, full moon ceremonies, equinoxes, all the alcohol and food-fuelled bacchanals they invented to bid farewell to one season and herald the next.

In our always on, 24/7, strawberries-in-winter-and-dine-at-dawn cities we've lost a lot of that connection. I like to structure my client contracts seasonally to make sure we aren't 'planting seeds' in summer or looking to 'harvest' in January.[1] Twelve weeks also turns out to be

---

1 My northern hemisphere clients.

a very natural work phase to get things done (not too long or short). Maybe that's why a season has come to be that length? Hmm.

Leaders know when you properly end a phase, it's far easier to create something new.

And if you feel there's nothing to celebrate, look again. If you're really appreciating what's happening you'll be grateful for each day, each breath. Even a 'lousy' day is one you've had the privilege of living. Even the most annoying colleague or customer is better than isolation. Appreciation is in short supply – certainly in the organisations I know. Recognising the end of things is a wonderful antidote to this.

Live like the story is going to end

It seems to me that the really inspiring leaders have figured out they, yes, will die. And this knowledge galvanises rather than debilitates them.

'Remembering that I'll be dead soon is the most important tool I've ever encountered to help me make the big choices in life', said Steve Jobs, 'because almost everything – all external expectation, all pride, all fear of embarrassment or failure – these things just fall away in the face of death, leaving only what is truly important'.

This was a leader who turned out to have less time than most people would expect – and achieved more than most people could possibly dream.

Elon Musk remember, doesn't just talk about retiring on Mars but dying there. Sadat went to the Knesset to make peace with Israel completely aware that this would likely lead to his assassination. Ghandi's willingness to put his own mortality on the line was a key to his power. Martin Luther King checked into the Lorraine Motel in Memphis well aware of the mortal risks he was running.

Closer to home (my home, that is) one of the most irrepressible humans I have ever met is Miha Pogacnik. Miha is a violinist who uses his instrument to seduce, stimulate and shake corporate audiences into a more awakened consciousness. He runs an extraordinary annual festival in a medieval Slovenian castle (the mythical birthplace of Parzival) that he has almost single-handedly rescued from ruin. He is the kind of man who runs a naval blockade to land a boat-full of artists in a besieged Dubrovnik. He has filled trains with creatives and criss-crossed Europe to bring the continent's attention to its shared cultural (and not just commercial) identity. And he once smuggled his violin into the pyramids to illicitly serenade the spirits of the sleeping pharaohs with Bach violin sonatas. He's a powerhouse who never seems to flag, however many obstacles he faces, or unsympathetic bureaucrats he has to woo, or funders he has to convince.

I used to wonder where he got his energy. What was his secret? One day he took me into a quiet room, opened his violin case and there, nestled next to his bows, was what I can only describe as a *memento mori*. I can't say exactly what I saw – because that would break a confidence – but let's just say every time Miha opens that case to play, he reminds himself of his mortality; life is finite and every day is valuable.

See ends as beginnings

So leaders embrace ends, including their own. And this enables them to think beyond. About who will succeed them. About the legacy they are creating. They are less inclined to think of themselves as owners, and more as stewards of a business, enterprise or organisation. They are writing personal stories that must end – but this ending generates new sequels, new beginnings.

The Hero's Journey is often depicted as a circle, not a line. The story doesn't take you from A to destination B. It delivers you back where you started (A2 you could say) an older and, hopefully, wiser person. Indeed the final scene of the classic hero's journey finds the protagonist returning home to be met by suspicion, resistance or outright hostility. As we know the *status quo* is not a fan of change.

Which is why, before long, the hero sets off on another story. The sequel. We can all think of stories we have lived that changed us. And made us itchy about returning to square one.

I like to think of the ongoing story – individual or collective – as a spiral. Each story brings you back to the same place but from a higher vantage point. You know more, you see more, you have evolved more. Round and round you go, not in a groove or rut, but an upward (hopefully) narrative spiral.

At each stage what makes you different is what you have learned.

Endings are educational

Stories are in their ancient essence a means of learning. From the earliest myths onwards, stories have been told and retold to teach us about our origins, our culture and our values.

A way to harvest the value of all the stories you've lived – including the ones you'd rather not have experienced – is to ask: what did I learn?

Looking through the learning lens, you have three main types of ending to choose from: comic, tragic and heroic.

In the comic ending the protagonist learns nothing and is doomed to repeat their mistakes for our entertainment. Don't confuse *comic* ending with *happy* ending. Comedies are delightful to watch but often hell to live. The comic protagonist is rarely transformed by the story into a wiser, more mature human. We want them to remain foolish and blinkered for our amusement. John Cleese's wonderful character, Basil Fawlty, may want Fawlty Towers to make it into the Michelin guide, but we'd hate it. We want to see him struggle and not achieve the dream. That's comedy.

In the tragic ending, the protagonist learns an important lesson but is too late to benefit from the wisdom. We, the audience, benefit from their tribulations and head out of the theatre or cinema gratified. And the hero floats down the river or wanders off into the wilderness.

And then, there's the heroic ending, where the protagonist(s) learn(s) in time to benefit from the insight. And is often then called to a new adventure.

If you are stuck for an end point to your future story, instead of asking *what do I want to achieve?* Try asking yourself *what do I want to learn?* And then construct your next future story around what you currently don't know, create one that will illuminate your blind spots and leave you not just older but wiser.

- So what kind of ending do you want for the future story you are currently authoring?
- Who benefits from this story, how is it bigger than yourself?
- How long are you giving yourself?
- What's beyond that story?
- And if your story ends with your life, what does it lead to?

The End?

So this is where we part company. But before we do, I want to return, in the best traditions of storytelling, to the beginning – and one final story.

Right at the start of the book, even before the pro-logue, there's a dedication to my father, Bernard Pearl. He knew I was dedicating this book to him. And he knew he wouldn't live to see it published. It sounds tragic but in truth it wasn't. I'm sad he isn't around, of course, but for a man of 85 to pass away surrounded by love, how and when he wanted, is heroic not tragic.

My father's end taught me a lot about endings.

He'd had a very accomplished life. He was born in 1930 to a working-class Jewish family in London's East End. It's a trendy part of town now – wall-to-wall artisan micro-breweries and selvedge denim – but in the '30s it was tough. But remember, in story there is always that action generating 'but'.

My dad was bright. And he loved learning. His CV is stellar. Youngest kid in his school to matriculate. One of the first to go to college. He became a dentist, then a barrister, then a coroner, then the head of the Mental Health Tribunal and head of a law chambers in Lincoln's Inn. On the way he picked up degrees in History and Philosophy and qualifications in Sociology and Forensic Odontology. 'Retirement' saw him take up Art which he studied and taught at the University of the Third Age. A real career to be proud of, packed with achievement.

But at the end, my father's mind wasn't on the achievement. It was all about the stories.

Stories full of emotion. Like the story of the mighty Russian cloth presser who tenderly placed my five-year-old dad on the trestle of his father's pattern cutting studio. Or the story of his first extraction as a young dental student. Or going down to Brighton to tell his father he'd become a barrister and watching the old tailor sob among his hydrangeas.

Stories about choice – about the doors he opened in life, and those he closed. About being offered his dream to become a doctor and listening to wise counsel instead. About studying law for fun and then suddenly realising – standing in Gray's Inn in his new wig and gown – that he actually wanted to practise as a lawyer. About the weekend he turned his back on the legal profession to save the strain on his family.

The good luck stories. He came to see his whole life as a stroke of luck. And the love stories. Sixty-three married years' worth.

It was all about the stories. The ones he created. The ones he lived.

My iPhone memory is stuffed with them. Our family gatherings are full of them. And what they teach me is it's not your achievements that outlive you, but your narrative. The stories you tell and the ones you live.

In the prologue of this book, I proposed what happens next is up to you. I feel the same.

We know that the stories we tell shape how we think, behave and treat each other. We understand that a well-crafted story creates meaning for others. And that this craft can be learned.

We have seen that humans are the Earth's great fiction makers. That fiction has been the driver of civilisation and progress. Our stories – for good and bad – have shaped the world we live in. And will continue to.

Understanding story gives great power. The power to engage. And enrage. The conflicts that are bubbling away in our organisations, and societies, are often fuelled by unhelpful stories. Stories of fear, fantasy and formula. And to replace these with something more helpful means coming up with better stories.

Right now we have the chance to author the story, not only of our lives, but our whole planet.

What happens next? That is up to us.

The End?

P.S.

 Those of us interested in democracy can't be distracted by the all divisive narratives out there but have to craft a collective story of our own. Books like David's can only help.

Lord Andrew Stone of Blackheath

I am writing this on New Year's Day 2017 and as this book goes into its first reprint. Looking back over the last year, I don't know whether to celebrate or apologise.

Let me explain.

I wrote this book as a guide to help leaders harness the power of story and to get things done, both now and in the future.

Since the book was first published in March 2016 two events stand out where story has been used to shape the world in ways that have taken us by surprise; the Brexit vote in Britain and the election of Donald Trump to the US Presidency.

As I write, the consequences of these events are not yet clear. Personally, I have my misgivings, but who knows, by the time you read this, we may all be living happily ever after in the rose-tinted futures the politicians promised. We shall see.

For now, I'd just like to reflect for a moment on the striking and, I feel, unprecedented way story was used in both cases to secure popular victories for improbable winners.

Brexit first. I talk in the book about the primal power of the scare story and both sides of the Brexit campaign did their very best to scare us into voting for them.[1]

The Remainers spent most of their energies painting a lurid picture of the economic Armageddon that would follow a Leave vote. They clearly assumed that rational self-preservation and fear of change would win the day. They were wrong. The Leavers countered by mocking 'Project Fear' for unpatriotic lack of courage and jumping

---

[1] In a binary, Yes/No referendum like this, the formidable complexities of the European question are polarised into two simplistic sides. Leavers and Remainers, Goodies and, depending on your point of view, Baddies. This has comic book appeal but is also highly divisive.

at shadows. In the same breath, the Eurosceptics seeded their own scare stories, graphically stoking the electorate's fear of immigration. They predicted a tsunami of unde-sirables inundating the country; hordes of work-shy, ne'er do wells hiding within their cadres of undercover terror-ists, sworn to destroy our democracy from within. Real disaster movie stuff. But they went one step further; *fear plus*, you could say.

Cleverly, the Leave camp's story-machine overlaid the horror narrative with lashings of fantasy, promising happily-ever-after outcomes where Brexit Britain gets to have its cake and eat it. As mentioned in the book, it's the over-simplicity of fantasies that make them both seductive and dangerous.

The Remainers tried to retaliate by exposing the Leave claims as fiction but to no avail. The Brexiteers had realised, as have many populist movements before them, that a frustrated, fearful population will prefer a simple fiction to a complex reality. As Leave.EU founder Arron Banks told The Independent immediately following the Leave win: 'The remain campaign featured fact, fact, fact, fact, fact. It just doesn't work. You have got to connect with people emotionally. It's the Trump success.'

Indeed. The clash of narratives that was the Brexit 'debate' was only a teaser for the full-out story war – the 'yarns race' – that was unfolding in America.

The US Presidential election is famously a media cir-cus, with the spoils often going to the candidate who best manages the popular medium of the day. When it came to swaying voters, Roosevelt completely understood the persuasive power of radio. JFK masterfully harnessed television. Obama engaged his base through Social Media. And the medium that allowed the ex-host of *The Apprentice* to wrest the election from the establishment's front-runner, Hillary Clinton?

Reality TV

In the first chapter of Story for Leaders, I talk about the ways in which story has, throughout human history, been an essential way for leaders to mobilize large groups of people to their cause. In the 21st century reality TV is a form of storytelling that perfectly suits the style and intentions of would-be leaders like Trump.

Firstly, as my dictionary tells me, it is 'a form of entertainment in which real people are continuously filmed and which is designed to be entertaining rather than informative'. Entertainment. The 'real people' are actually talent spotted, auditioned and hired as cast. The continuous filming is heavily edited. The spontaneity is scripted, the 'true confessions' rehearsed. Reality TV is every bit as artificially stage managed as a Hollywood movie – just a lot cheaper. And the man even some Republicans are calling the 'Entertainer in Chief' knows this well.

Secondly, reality TV thrives on conflict, outburst and confrontation. The kind of vitriol that was off limits to professional politicians even a few years ago is the stock in trade of the reality TV star. It's how Trump and his kind keep the public and the media tuned in, returning night after night to see what new outrage has been committed.

Thirdly, many people feel alienated from the political process and powerless to influence its leaders. Reality TV feeds our desire for special access, a backstage pass to what's *really* happening. It offers illusions that Big Brother is talking directly to us and that we are hearing the unmediated truth from the horse's mouth. By the standards of reality TV Trump is a man who 'tells it like it is'. In reality, just like other future-hackers, *he tells it like he wants us to think it is*. The audience may feel they are being taken into the leader's confidence. They are actually just being taken in.

And most important of all, though it purports to be documentary, reality TV is actually *fiction*. As an audience, we know this and don't mind. It's phony, so what? We enjoy the truth-lite world where unknowns get to be pop idols, where Cinderella meets her billionaire bachelor Prince Charming, where a hard-working, plucky apprentice passes a series of ordeals to be finally awarded the job of a lifetime. Since we crouched around the primal fireside, humans have yearned for fairy tale endings. We don't really expect them to come true. And we don't hold the storyteller to task if they don't happen. Applying this same principle to the electoral process – as we saw this year – encourages candidates to concoct wildly overblown future stories (these used to be called lies) but frees them from accountability if they fail to deliver.

When Trump proclaimed he would lock Hillary up or reboot coal-mining, he wasn't talking policy in the conventional sense, he was telling stories designed to stimulate, provoke and, where useful, put us to sleep.

It's a Humpty Dumpty world where the southern border of the nation is to be magically protected by a 'great, great wall' that not only keeps Mexican migrants out (clearly this is a story where the tunnel or ladder has yet been invented), but which the Mexicans also fund.

We will see how many of these promises are kept.[2] If they are not, will the electorate be surprised? I doubt it. Did we really think they were genuine in the first place? Any more than we believe celebrities are truly stranded in the jungle, or the Real Housewives of Atlanta are in any meaningful way real?

Welcome to the 'post-truth' world[3]

The Brexit and Trump phenomena are not isolated – they are just the two most vivid examples of storytelling

---

[2] At a post-election rally, Trump actually chided his supporters for chanting the campaign's battle-cry of 'Lock her Up!' explaining 'No, no. That doesn't play well after a victory'.

[3] Watch out when the media use this phrase and talk about 'fake news' as though prior to this, the news was truthful. As you'll read in the book, we've always been living in a post-truth world. It is just that today this is more glaringly obvious than ever before.

or what I call Authoring the Future in action. And we are likely to see a lot more in the coming years. Emboldened by the success of brazen fibbers like Farage, Boris Johnson and The Donald, other unscrupulous leaders-to-be are no doubt crafting their own fear, fantasy and formula narratives aimed straight at our most primal neurology.

Hence my mixed feelings as we reprint *Story for Leaders*. While I am happy the book is being widely read, I am uneasy about how the technology I describe in it is open to misuse. I don't expect my book has directly contributed to these world-shaping events. But if it did, in any way – sorry.

Equally, narrative has never been a more potent global currency, making this the perfect time to harness the power of story for good.

And that's why this preface ends not with celebration or apology but an invitation.

The best way to counter unhelpful stories is to come up with something better. I invite you to use the techniques in this book to create narratives that are more persuasive than the dark primal myths currently on offer.

Story is a power tool. I invite you to be mindful about what you want to build with it.

I invite you to be vigilant about the narratives you hear and selective about those you choose to believe to be true. Question who is trying to hack your future and what they stand to gain from it. Broaden your diet of news and current affairs so you get the richest, most nuanced narrative to base your decisions.[4]

I invite you to manage the story making abilities of your mind to keep things in perspective. I've already talked about perspective in the book but just notice how often we are told that doom is imminent, time has run out, that we are near to 'breaking point'. The tight deadline is a storytelling technique designed to build tension. It can galvanise your listeners but it may also kill creativity, discourage innovation and stifle action with fear. When you are authoring your own future – and that of your teams and organisations – I invite you to break the tempo of the daily news cycle, the weekly numbers and the quarterly report and create longer-term stories that carry us to the horizon and beyond.

I invite you to think of yourself not only as a storyteller but a meaning maker. This is a confusing world and the people in it crave meaning. When you create that meaning you radically shape how people around you think and act.

---

[4] I thought it was striking that in his interview (with Rolling Stone Magazine) the day after the Trump win, the outgoing President Obama made it clear he was not going to disappear from public life but after a short holiday and a year of book writing was planning to return with a mission: 'How do we rethink our storytelling, the messaging and use of digital media, so that we can make a persuasive case across the country?'

And finally, I warmly invite you to use this book and everything in it to create stories you'll be inspired to tell and proud to live.

David Pearl
Piedmont, Italy
1st January 2017

ABOUT

People often ask me what I do – not least my mother. I usually end up telling them what I've *done*. Music. Opera. TV. Theatre. Directing. Writing. Advertising. Consulting. Experience Engineering.

I think I missed school the day they told us we could only live one story per life!

Today I describe myself as an innovator in business, the arts and social change. That includes working with some of the world's leading organisations – and those who lead them – helping them discover the stories they really want to tell and live.

My story is unfolding just as yours is. If you want to compare notes or would appreciate some help kick-starting your next chapter, you can find me at:

w: www.davidpearl.net

e: info@pearlgroup.net

t: +44 (0)20 8099 5154

🐦: @DavidPearlHere

**LONDON
BUSINESS
FORUM**

I have designed, led and spoken at more events around the world than I can remember. And there's no-one quite like **London Business Forum**. If you want real inspiration, from world-class speakers, in a format that's fun and fits easily into your work week, you'll want to check out their programme.

They encouraged me to write this book and they've made it possible. So massive thanks for that! Also, if you want to buy bulk copies of *Story for Leaders*, especially if you would like to customise them with your company logo, then the team at London Business Forum would be delighted to hear from you:

w: www.londonbusinessforum.com

e: info@londonbusinessforum.com

t: +44 (0)20 7600 4222

🐦: @LBFEvents